Ernő Szép

The Smell of Humans
A MEMOIR OF THE HOLOCAUST IN HUNGARY

Translated by John Bátki
With an introductory essay by Dezső Tandori

CENTRAL EUROPEAN UNIVERSITY PRESS
Budapest · London · New York

First published in Hungarian as *Emberszag* in 1945 by
Keresztes, Budapest

Reprinted in 1984 by Szépirodalmi Könyvkiadó, Budapest

© Ernő Szép Estate 1984

First published in English as *The Smell of Humans* in 1994
English translation copyright © CEU Press 1994
Introduction copyright © Dezső Tandori 1994

British Library Cataloguing in Publication Data
A CIP catalogue record for this book is available from the British Library

ISBN 1-85866-014-9 Hardback
ISBN 1-85866-011-4 Paperback

Library of Congress Cataloging in Publication Data
A CIP catalog record for this book is available from the Library of Congress

Published by
Central European University Press
H-1021 Budapest, Hűvösvölgyi út 54
Distributed by
Oxford University Press, Walton Street, Oxford OX2 6DP
Oxford New York Athens Auckland Bangkok Bombay
Calcutta Cape Town Dar es Salaam Delhi Florence Hong Kong
Istanbul Karachi Kuala Lumpur Madras Madrid Melbourne
Mexico City Nairobi Paris Singapore Taipei Tokyo Toronto
and associated companies in Berlin Ibadan
Distributed in the United States
by Oxford University Press Inc., New York

Design and typesetting by John Saunders
Printed and bound in Great Britain by Biddles of Guildford

Contents

ERNŐ SZÉP

Autobiographical Statement (1947)

I was born in 1884, but my life began before that: my father was a teacher who learned to play the violin very beautifully, and my mother was such a sensitive soul that in the springtime the first peeps of the newly hatched chicks were enough to bring tears to her eyes. I think that's where the music I made in poems comes from, including the impulse that drove me to write poems.

I went to school in Hajdúszoboszló, Debrecen, Mezőtúr and Budapest.

I don't know why people feel compelled to describe their schooling even in the briefest résumé. One's life history shows in one's thinking. What took place in my head constitutes my life; the other things that happened to me were not really my doing and do not belong to me.

I had many beautiful thoughts, believe me; so much I would have liked to write would have made more worthwhile reading than what I did write. My God, if you could only read the poems I never wrote. I always needed the money, so I wrote feuilletons, I wrote articles, I wrote cabaret songs, plays; I wrote novels and I wrote filmscripts that nobody bought.

I, too, labour under a delusion that I am getting younger by the day, and will have the money at last to begin what I had planned, so that I can lie in peace in my grave, having accomplished what was entrusted to me: publishing my whole heart.

JOHN BÁTKI

Introduction

Budapest, 20 October 1944. Ernő Szép, the 60-year-old
Hungarian Jewish poet, playwright and novelist, is among the
fifty elderly men wearing the yellow star who are brutally
rounded up from the apartment building on Pozsonyi Road by
gun-toting Arrow Cross youths, and marched off into the
unknown. *The Smell of Humans* is the story of the next nineteen
days, narrated with a remarkable degree of compassion and detach-
ment by a master of twentieth-century Hungarian literature.

Ernő Szép was born on 30 June 1884 in Huszt, in the eastern part of the Austro-Hungarian empire, and grew up in a small
town in eastern Hungary, where his father was a schoolteacher,
and his mother a seamstress. From these humble origins, starting
with his 1902 volume of poems *Első csokor* ('First Bouquet'), he
went on to a career as a popular writer in Budapest who would
publish well over thirty volumes of poetry, fiction and plays, end-
ing with the 1945 appearance of *Emberszag* ('The Smell of
Humans'). Already before the First World War Szép had gained

recognition as one of the writers grouped around the pioneering literary periodical *Nyugat* ('West'), dominated by the personality of his slightly older contemporary, the epoch-making poet Endre Ady. For a variety of reasons Ernő Szép's critical reputation during his lifetime and after his death in 1953 was that of an outstanding poet in the 'minor' mode. This picture has changed considerably with the advent of Dezső Tandori, who, since the late 1970s, in a series of essays and a volume of selections from Szép's poetry and prose, has single-handedly created an entirely new level of Ernő Szép appreciation for generations to come. Even more significantly, Tandori's own poetry and prose, considered by some to be the most significant Hungarian literary oeuvre of the late twentieth century, has consistently included generous portions of Szép's work, in the form of allusion, direct and indirect quotation, 'subtext' and leitmotif. Tandori has, in fact, resurrected an author who was in danger of falling into a 'black hole' of his nation's collective conscience and memory.

For nearly forty years after the event, the fact of the Holocaust eluded full public confrontation and examination in Hungary. It is no accident that *The Smell of Humans*, written and originally published in 1945, was not reissued in Hungary until 1984 (the year that saw the publication of Tandori's volume of selections from Szép). Ambivalence persists to this day about collective responsibility for the destruction of Hungarian Jewry.

By the time of the events narrated in *The Smell of Humans* (October–November 1944), the 'organized' brunt of the Holocaust had already transpired. After the German occupation of Hungary on 19 March, hundreds of thousands of Jews were rounded up in ghettos all over the country. Edmund Veesenmayer, Hitler's minister plenipotentiary in Budapest, reported that (under Eichmann's command) 437,402 Jewish men, women and children were transported to Auschwitz between 14 May and 8 July. Some 230,000 Jews remained in Budapest, in daily terror of their lives.

The fate of the Budapest Jewry hung in a tragic balance during the summer of 1944. Against the SS, ever demanding and ready to carry out further deportations, the waning powers of the aged Governor Horthy proved only partially effective in protecting the Jewish population. (The community of about 3,000 Jews in the outlying Budapest district of Újpest was rounded up and packed into cattle-wagons overnight; on 17 July the 1,500 mostly Jewish prisoners at the Kistarcsa camp were also seized and abducted to Auschwitz after the Governor's intervention had seemingly saved them.) During these months representatives of neutral states – Sweden, Switzerland, Portugal and Spain – offered some hope of shelter by issuing protective passes and establishing 'protected houses'. The heroic efforts of Raoul Wallenberg saved thousands of lives.

On 15 October, as Russian troops approached Budapest, Governor Horthy made an ill-prepared attempt to withdraw Hungary from the war by declaring on Hungarian Radio a unilateral cessation of hostilities. On the same day he was deposed by German troops, and the government was seized by the extremist Arrow Cross party led by Szálasi. Instead of surrendering, the Germans and their Hungarian allies made desperate efforts to defend the city, sending thousands of Jewish slave labourers, Ernő Szép among them, to dig earthworks around the outskirts of Budapest. The Russians reached the perimeter on 6 November, but the ensuing bloody siege of Budapest ended only on 13 February. During these months of hell the Arrow Cross thugs went on a murderous rampage against the defenceless wearers of the yellow star. Ernő Szép, after his dismissal from forced labour on 6 November, miraculously managed to survive the siege and the reign of terror. Not so his brothers József and Márton, murdered, and his sister Vilma, 'disappeared'. And let us not forget the fate of the remaining members of Szép's forced labour company, who were not dismissed on 6 November, and were probably driven west along with retreating Hungarian army units. It was on such a forced march, and around this time, that the great Hungarian Jewish poet Miklós Radnóti was murdered: his last poem is dated 31 October 1944.

After the war, with the exception of *The Smell of Humans*, Ernő Szép published only shorter, occasional pieces in periodicals. He was not in favour among the Marxist literary policy-makers who came into power in the late 1940s, nor did he in any way participate in the Stalinist programme of literary manifestations. He died in Budapest in October 1953. The publication of this memoir, and a future volume of selected poetry and prose, will, I trust, introduce a new friend (as Tandori says in his introductory essay, an 'unknown familiar') to readers everywhere.

DEZSŐ TANDORI
'Please Forgive Me...'

Ernő Szép, the Unknown Familiar

Ernő Szép remains to this day a debt owed not only by Hungarian literature, but world literature as well.

Or should I say, we all owe him? Me too, oh yes, even though supposedly I've tried 'to do a lot for him'.

It was easy – it came from the heart. And that's the part, the bodily organ, that best defines Ernő Szép, if we wanted to characterize him.

Surely, it is easy to rely on the heart, for one who's been blessed/cursed by the gods with such sharp wits and eyes. Our great writer Kosztolányi, who is not entirely unknown in the world at large, says somewhere that compassion indeed ought to reside in the *sharp* light of our eyes.

Ernő Szép's eyes, so often misting over, still flash with such bright sharpness at all his human objects, titbits of nature, lifeless existence; at beer-mug, cloud, sparrow. He is a great contemporary, not only of the Hungarian writer above-mentioned, but a coeval and equal of T. S. Eliot, at times anticipating Kafka, as I have documented in detail elsewhere (in vain?) . . . so much so that I doubt I could recall it all here . . . but never mind, I don't mean to belabour the reader with proofs and sworn statements – for Ernő Szép, unhappiness was easy. Everything was easy for him, for he had 'purchased the tickets' – tokens of a most infinitesimally precise spiritual sensibility – to some of the most important 'lines' in the world: walkways and riversides, the trails left by migrating insects; the arc inscribed, on its way to the ground, by a tiny bit of bark snapping off from a tree-trunk; or the way smoke rises, motes tremble in sunlight; the miracle of aerial spaces . . . the dying violin tone.

For us – and from now on, perhaps for English-language readers too – it was like a virtuoso god, the way he, Sir Ernő, struck up and also how he ceased to play.

He left an emptiness behind as great as William Carlos Williams's sparrow, who was sung by Ernő Szép as well, the dead sparrow whose crop had been trodden upon by a horse, or flattened by an automobile tyre . . . so that only an escutcheon remains, sort of, a heraldic effigy on the pavement.

It was this kind of heraldry of human existence that Ernő Szép knew so well. This is what he wrote about when he reassured his future reader (in modern versions of the French alexandrines), 'You who stroll the walkway a hundred years from now': it's for you – yes, that's how he addresses us – it's for you that I want to tell . . . what? What does he want, what does he need to tell? That he exhaled breath with a soft 'Ha' sound, that he had heard about God (the power that gave him speech!), and that we're here to die. 'I see,' he says. Whereas he doesn't even know what is to be done (he writes, in the 1910s!!!): if he only knew who is most beautiful, what is the best thing, what is to be done.

That is the kind of stuff he writes, in easily translatable, stone-simple poems, that he just keeps walking, stopping – whereabouts . . .? On streets and squares . . . Yes, as if we were to see this little man in a video clip, say, in snowy New York, or, as an Englishman, say, in Kensington; yes, there he walks with me, and when thinking of him brings tears to my eyes, as now . . . It's as if he said: stop that, no sentimentality, please. He, Ernő Szép, was so tough, exacting and forgivingly sensitive *in our stead, too*, as if he had run countless errands for us . . .

. . . and had warned us countless times about how much we've left undone.

We have a myriad things to do, Ernő Szép tells us, a myriad within a human lifespan that no one bothered to teach us how to live out. How, indeed? How do we do it? Insects know their business, how to be insects. Birds know. The mote of dust, the flower – they all know. Whereas he *wavers* so, as he writes in a poem. (Oh, I would love to help someone translate his poems; it would be incredibly easy . . . all you need is a little knowledge of obvious English, and as additional help there is Ernő Szép himself, making it so easy to love him!) This constant, seeming helplessness of his provides an elemental momentum . . .

. . . in a world such as this, fifty, sixty, seventy years after the birth of his works, in an era full of supposedly marvellous inventions . . . as Byron writes sarcastically, 'for killing bodies, and for saving souls,/all propagated with the best intentions'.

Ernő Szép never mocks. His vast, all-understanding sense of humour is full of insight, an intuition that is also a seeing-into-it, and one that he does not show off. As I said, he would prefer to compare himself to a poor 'stiff', staggering like a drunk in the streetcar (or these days let's say bus, or subway, etc.), unable to *stand still*, no matter how hard he grabs the strap. His shorthand expressions are legendary (among the circles of his aficionados), for instance the way he simply announces: I can't stand still. As if this also meant: standing one's ground, *being* upright, standing tall in the storm . . . and why can't we be, why can't we live, evidently, in the world? For we must ask the trees, that's right, how it is done . . . and they surely know (writes Ernő Szép, his innocent knowledge anticipating by several decades those notables of Hungarian literature who 'discovered' such things way after him). The trees know all sorts of things, they ought to whisper to us 'something lucidly beautiful', because we . . . but no, no! Ernő Szép says I, meaning himself, Ernő Szép: because I . . . we, he, I, cannot *adjust* ourselves, himself, myself *to life*. As Rilke puts it in his *Orpheus* poem: 'We have no knowledge of each other.'

It is this mysterious language, on a par with Rilke's, that Ernő Szép *sounded*, while he wrote poems.

But he is just as much at home in prose.

He 'cultivated' the poem without any pretences – his was always the prime prose of natural poetic speech, a simplicity spiced with mysteries, a delicacy unveiled in its incredibly natural being . . . this was his world.

He stuns his reader by leading to stunning realization. Just like that. Something, anything, it makes no difference what. What Ernő Szép tells us at any one time could fit into the ongoing great Hamlet-monologue of life on earth. In a way so that he himself, like the donor in old paintings, stands captured for all time, a tiny figure in a corner of the picture.

Or not even there. Merely his name, like a memorial, written above the poem or prose piece. And what does he talk about in his prose and poetry? He tells us to believe only the good, the only truth; 'one dawn' we'll find all the horrors of the world gone, even though the newspaper insists on detailing all those monstrosities; oh, no, what truly EXISTS is: 'thank you, please, oh, how nice', this is what exists, and the plethora of neckties (all those goods) glittering in the shop-windows, on seeing which we blame ourselves for not taking advantage of all these possibilities, for not being able to live in other people's outfits, bodies and souls, yes, and Ernő Szép says all of this as if he were unaware he was expecting the impossible from us, humans . . . as if he didn't know better than anyone that we mustn't delude ourselves. He has no illusions, yet loves miracles: this is the miracle of Ernő Szép. This is what makes it possible to love him.

And what does it mean, 'to love'? What do I mean by this, I who am a somewhat medieval-knightly 'sparrow-royalist' who learned even this self-definition from Ernő Szép, borrowed, inhaled it, through so many hidden layers, through so much devotion? What does it mean for me, this devotion to Ernő Szép's oeuvre?

Simply this: I try to speak of him by way of tiny details. I do not try to make my task easier (I don't want to alienate him!) by attempting to summarize him in grand 'concepts'. I feel that of all people on earth, I, at least, would not succeed (and this is my victory!) – no way could I succeed with such a summing-up. I can only piece together, detail by tiny detail, that gossamer-mosaic, capturing what? What am I able to hand over to you?

And by the way, you must know that what I have said is his, Ernő Szép's, gift, to me. That I am able to play around like this, in an aggressive world. Where – and he, too, knew this, only he was more courteous than I, he was always 'blaming himself', 'swallowing his tears', wanting 'to deserve' the joy of sleep, so that he could sit down on his own bed, next to his dead body, his own dead figure, yes, just like an understanding friend who wanted to learn and keep each word of the dead man – yes, I am able to poke gentle fun in his name, thanks to him, in a world where, in the case of filthy turns of events (while we are powerless!), supposedly (really?) we ought to feel responsible . . . although we have recognized that we don't even yet know what it takes to live as human beings.

I do not want to comment here either on 'Sarajevo' or on 'Auschwitz-and-neighbourhood'. I would rather merely say that Kafka, of *The Penal Colony* . . . Kafka, of *The Hunger Artist*, the definite article capitalized, signifying a universal concept, something unique . . . Kafka's intonation, for instance, in a more tender version, lurks there, at times anticipating Kafka, in Ernő Szép's way of thinking and sensibility. T. S. Eliot's *Prufrock*, and the non-avantgarde overtones of *The Waste Land*, are also present in Sir Ernő's poetry. He is, at the very least, there in a photo-finish along with these greats, these immortals whose miracle remains incomprehensible to this day.

Is this what I want to say about him? Is this what I have to give him?

No, no. He would protest. He would ask, what evidence do I have to support my overconfidence in him?

Yes, how can I say things like that about him? About Ernő Szép, who asks to be forgiven – in a litanied, incantatory poem of vigil – by every living creature even less perfect, more fallible, more prone to fall than himself (see Beckett, *All That Fall* . . . oh, so Sir Ernő is a forerunner of Beckett's view of human existence as well . . . only thing is, he never exploited these things to that extent, elegantly concealing his suffering and his fear of one-sidedness, preferring to abandon himself to a worse fate for not having evolved a 'trademark character' so essential in Western art. Although Hungarian literature, too, has belonged to the realm of Western art, since the years just before the First World War – it was no accident that *Nyugat* ('West') was the name of the loftily European periodical and literary movement that enlist-ed the most select writers of the day . . . it is no accident that a whole line of subsequent Hungarian writers (our immediate pre-decessors) gave easy access for many of us to become Europeans and 'citizens of the world', even if this is not known about us by the inhabitants of that republic or 'kingdom' to which we should not even have to long for admission . . . where, thanks to Ernő Szép and his like, we are already represented . . . just as we, too, have a share in the city of Dublin (and not merely at 'second hand', as hand-me-downs from Joyce and Beckett, but if! say I, but if! how nice to have this 'if '. . . Ernő Szép provides us, from the word go, with our own Continental base, then we might as well go island-hopping, no?), by the Round Pond in Kensington Gardens, alongside the one and only, the 'great' Murphy – not the commercial substitute! – we mind dachshunds for our basic wherewithal, goliard-like, metropolitan vagrants . . . so let me close my parentheses, Ernő Szép would like that), he who asks to be forgiven by all the aggrieved and humiliated; this makes him a disciple of Dostoevsky and Tolstoy, that's right, and a forerunner of Beckett and company. I have already said whose coeval and equal he is.

Well Mr Ernő Szép would like this even less; he would not dare to condemn this gesture of mine (for fear of offending me!), but he would find the means to . . . no, not even to refute my opinion that he actually belongs among the greats of world literature, no, he would merely point out, by means of a few artlessly plain verses, words critical of his own clothes, way of life, his 'frivolous', feeble understanding . . . what would he point out? Like a slip of the pen, a typo, a poorly inscribed character in Kafka – according to Kafka, etc. – as Salinger quotes (conjures) it for sketching his Seymour, stands as a witness that the writer is indeed a very poor writer, that you are most certainly at fault, says Kafka, says Ernő Szép. He (our Ernő Szép) shares and suffers Prufrock's bad conscience for having abandoned someone who might die in the meantime, and how could he ever forgive himself? – recall that Eliot has his hero asking: should he have the right to smile? Well, that is how Ernő Szép asks our forgiveness in advance, that's right, as if we were standing on the stage of *Godot*, raising our paws, human-animal-inseparabilities, beings on earth, essentials – therefore pitiable; pitiable, therefore capable of understanding pitiability; therefore pitying, hearts filled with endless sorrow and pity. But Ernő Szép is never sentimental, with him it's not sorrow and tears . . . What, then?

Poems and prose, of the highest polish, and still tossed off with the grace of a laughing aristocrat. A stream of thoughts . . . a thought . . . a phrase . . . an orphaned word . . . a sound . . . a thought that floats away like smoke, even if we're forever thinking, even if we pause on a bridge and look down. (The way he could pause on a bridge, to watch the water! The way he could muse about why indeed does one watch the water so much . . . and why should we wonder, he says in one of the introductory poems of his oeuvre, around the turn of the century, why should we be so amazed by bare trees? Perhaps to sense autumn-drawn mysteries, whispered by intertangled twigs? And how was he supposed to untangle it all, what to do with the message? Like the latter-day son in Delmore Schwartz's story, in his dream at the movies seeing his poor parents, doomed to torment each other, about to help him into this world; given their dire straits, into an unhappy world where the succession of responsibilities already begins in dreams, a world where already in our dreams we are summoned – *In Dreams Begin Responsibilities* . . . that's right, in the early Sixties when I was a mere pup of a writer, a novelist called Géza Ottlik, one of Kosztolányi's rare, worthy successors, told me about American fiction, the long and short of it, and encouraged me to translate precisely the story mentioned above, by Delmore Schwartz, which I ended up translating . . . and how many times since then have I seen Delmore Schwartz, in airport waiting areas, accidentally gleaned newspapers, the photo taken not long before he died, yes, shortly before his death, as he sits on a bench, already way beyond this world . . . It always makes me think of Ernő Szép right away, Szép, who, as it were, shed off, moulted off entire worlds, and in the end said, summarizing the meaning of his life, resigned, but still courageous: 'I used to be Ernő Szép.' This is how he introduced himself, they say.

And meanwhile he meant to be accurate/exacting like Delmore Schwartz's boardwalk photographer, the absolute artist cast up by destiny at the Coney Island Amusement Park . . . seeing those two certified lunatics, the Young Man and the Girl, about whom one could already have foretold back then that their life together would only be misery, something which the boy, their son – waking up at the dream movie theatre – knows, knows, knows – and weeps for . . . and I no longer know, no longer want to know (is this a nonchalant, Ernő Szép-type elegance? or a sparrow-kingdom insouciance? etc.) how this sentence began; I am going to let myself be bowled over backwards by helplessness, the sacred hopelessness of *soul to soul travel*, I allow it to happen ('*let it be*' thought!) – Ernő Szép, Delmore Schwartz, Kafka, let all those about to fall, be thought. Whose forgiveness our Sir Ernő beseeched with such genteel elegance.

In Dublin, if, having just emerged from stylish buildings I find myself walking among green garbage bins, it is via Ernő Szép's universe, the sudden miracle of a warehouse street smelling of fish, that a Beckett atmosphere 'clicks in'.

Or else this is how I am able to follow Joyce on some of his rambles, encountering one of his figures not merely as a literary *tour de force*, but in actual personal proximity . . .

This is how I sense what this Ernő Szép book gives/tells us: the true 'smell of humans'. Alas, Ernő Szép himself knew the frailty of human appearance, human motion, human will, human thought . . . and smell, too . . . frail, for we ourselves are just that, that is – forgive me! – it is almost as if he himself shouldered the world's faults, and were begging the world's forgiveness for his existence and his suffering, which was still not enough to redeem anyone, for who is he, after all?

Who am I, to do anything significant for Ernő Szép?

All I can do is tell about him, try to recite him. By now, looking at me from his sky, perhaps seeing some passable morsel of my efforts, he shakes his head with a forbearing smile.

And he apologizes to me, for making me go through all this effort for him!

And he would ask the world, in this memoir/diary, in this book so full of war: would that it stopped this madness.

He would ask the same of today's world. He would embrace Mandela instead of 'marvelling' at the man's statue, of course, at the fact that Glasgow has a public square named after Mandela . . . yes, I have seen parks and statues like that, response-signs of the efforts towards forgiveness and reconciliation, and often thought of Ernő Szép.

Everything he wanted to ask of heaven on behalf of a people, a nation, a homeland, he put into a prayer – in his poem
'Prayer', which is folk-song-like, making him a predecessor (even
if they did not want to notice this!) of the latter-day offshoot of
folk poetry, and a champion of the patriotic lyric – but who wanted to see this little old man in that light?

Many of us see him like that, and smile with even greater
love – again, what would he say hearing this! Probably that he
didn't deserve it.

And yet he was so many things, both at the basic and at
the highest levels . . . there he stands at so many new beginnings
(in poetry and prose; I know little about the theatre and will not
speak of his plays; they say he has an important and beautiful
dramatic oeuvre – but I will stick to the things I know a little bit
about, to tell you who he was . . .), yes, there he stands at so
many new beginnings of twentieth-century Hungarian literature; he is like Gogol's renowned overcoat. Except that still there
are many who refuse to notice him.

I am happy that one fine day (Szép – the name he received
or adopted, I don't know – means 'fine' in Hungarian, isn't that a
sweet touch?) Mr Ernő Szép sounded the wake-up call for me
(obviously against his will! But can I be sure? When one of his
finest poems, the one with the soft 'Ha' exhalations, is titled 'This
Is for You', I've already mentioned it! Well then? It's complicated,
so very complicated, isn't it?), he woke me up: you, my man, are
wealthy . . .! For here I am, existing for you . . .! Here I am . . .

Well, this claim of mine would definitely make him angry.

Angry? He couldn't be. He even apologized to the sparrows, as he watched them in the park by the casino on the island
in the Danube (where he, the 'wealthy' human, possessor of an
entire kaiser roll, was 'idling', doing nothing!), he apologized for
throwing them too large a crumb, which one sparrow must have
especially taken to his poor heart, for he struggled so much with
that hopelessly large crumb (I would add, like Sisyphus with his
rock), and obviously this sparrow would not have an easy night's

rest now, and who knows what other troubles would therefore befall him . . . troubles all caused by him, Ernő Szép, this human with his fumbling goodwill . . . in other words, even our goodwill is so awkward, so rough-hewn, says he . . . apologizing practically in the name of all humankind to this disquieted sparrow.

Oh, God, is that it? As Hamlet would say: 'There's a special providence in the fall of a sparrow' (dear translator, please, look this up . . .); but a great Hungarian poet rendered this as 'a young sparrow', 'not even a young sparrow falls without the will of Providence'. And then our Ernő Szép, probably not thinking of Hamlet, casually scores a bull's-eye here, too . . . and he has hundreds of such bull's-eyes about life. And where he does not (as, for instance, one doesn't find them everywhere in this book; yes, his prose could be represented at a much higher level by some future selection, made, I trust, with similarly noble intentions, just as this present book finds its way to the reader's table not primarily because of aesthetic considerations, but because of a *worldwide need*; it is a necessity of life, essential as bread itself . . .): I implore the reader, like that sparrow, please do not judge Mr Ernő Szép from this large mouthful, but – am I being ridiculous? I ask you to please write me letters in your solitary hours, if you, dear reader, feel any such solitude that could possibly be helped by Ernő Szép, by corresponding with someone about Ernő Szép, go ahead please, I have been living here for 55 years, as Doderer says in his poem engraved on Viennese steps, 'amid wars'; this is the 56th year I've lived here . . . and my address, in the interest of letters to be written about Mr Ernő Szép is: 1013 Budapest I., Lánchíd u. 23. III.3., Hungary . . . And let me apologize to the book's translator, who in my opinion did terrific work, apologies to this man who did devoted work, and to whom I still owe an 'Ernő Szép memorial walk', which will surely take place, so, to make amends, happy amends, I make this promise that I am willing to correspond about Ernő Szép . . .

. . . please state your requests, what kinds of poems and prose pieces should I find for you in Sir Ernő's oeuvre, and in my poor English or German, or my more tolerable but still poor Hungarian, I will write back whatever I can, on Ernő Szép's behalf.

Perhaps he'd be less likely to be angry about this: that to help out the evening sparrow I, poorer than a sparrow, use as my means him, who holds himself to be even poorer.

One can always use a blessing that was 'provoked' by such means!

So has Ernő Szép turned me into a calculating person? Is this how he became my master? By giving me the gift of his life's work, me among others, to do whatever I will with it?

Even so, absolutely.

Unconditionally.

Without conditions. He gives himself. But after all – he did so long ago! Didn't he? By putting into words . . .

What did he put into words?

Only that which floats off as smoke, wrinkles as human skin, lingers miserably, balefully as snipped curls in a locket . . .

No need to go on.

That flattened sparrow. The scorched butterfly. The freshly gelded animal. The blinded ones. Enough of that. The smell of humans.

But no, let's not leave off.

Let's not stop at asking their forgiveness. Oh, God . . . does such forgiveness even exist? So great a forgiveness? The forgiveness of all those dead, who . . .

But why probe what exists and what doesn't. That is not what literature dwells on; it does not look for causal explanations to this question. What literature wants is for us somehow to swing across that otherwise insurmountable *gap*, or hitch, etc. Against all odds. Towards our own next moment. Which we'll somehow have to live through. As human beings. So that it does not stink with an evil smell.

Humans, that's what we have to be. But how? Even if we air out all the stink.

Or if the kind of prose and poetry gets written . . .

. . . only I can say this, about him – such as Ernő Szép's. Catharsis, we have this ancient word for it. This memoir/diary is a cathartic work.

One diminutive man, seized, dragged off, driven away to be slaughtered, gives an account of how he lived through it, and – past it.

Past it . . . but of course he does not overdo it. The sharp light of his eye reflects pity felt for humans. For ourselves.

He does not settle for anything less.

Why is he such a treasure – so valuable, and *dear, dear* – our Mr Ernő Szép? *Ernest Dear*, why, tell me? Because he does not settle for anything less. No way can we call him submissive . . .! Solid, tenacious, tough, yes. His eyes carry clearly. This is a word-play in my language, possibly translatable: his eyes carry far, see distance as clear as near, and also carry what they see, bearing the burden of the seen. Under that weight this small man is bent over, this small man who asks the sparrow's forgiveness.

So naturally I call myself a sparrow, and feel that I am the citizen of an entire kingdom – we want a nice French word here! the French name, not for exile, but for kingdom, *royaume*! – free-thinking citizen of the Royal Sparrow Republic, a subject who is not subject to feeling inferior to anyone, because he is the one Mr Ernő Szép has apologized to.

And from now on if they ask me who am I, why am I travelling here, what do I want, I am going to reply – and most definitely to the heavenly *immigration officer*! – 'Well sir, I happen to be the sparrow that Mr Ernő Szép apologized to . . . and I, not out of crude reciprocation, but for other reasons, choose to sing his praises.'

But what kind of glory can a sparrow proclaim? I would want to do just that, and I would be delighted if my words had precisely that effect. Then I would have succeeded in telling what a great writer I am offering here – for all of world literature. To be read, and let's leave it at that.

The rest remains to be seen.

I hope so! As I said:

my address is:

Dezső Tandori

1013 Budapest . . .

as stated above. If you want to find my address and only glance here at the end of this writing, you will have to look into my text, which came into being solely for Ernő Szép's sake. And so my work was not in vain. I can say that this is what I was.

No matter how much Ernő Szép protests, I will admit: I was happy to be him, occasionally, for a little while.

That is one conceivable alternative self-identity in the world. True literature, great or small, exists for this end. And so I often carry about me Ernő Szép's selected works.

To be read, and leave it at that.

Amid whatever wars.

With enough mercy for ourselves in our hearts to believe that it is possible to strive towards the kind of work that Ernő Szép, possibly, did not even especially strive for.

Let him be for us, in times of trouble, our longed-for, dreamed-for endeavour towards grace.

Like Mr Delmore's boardwalk photographer for that dreaming boy. That's how we should be for ourselves. Even if we were also to be that poor, inane girl or that young man. Even so.

With this, I take my leave. *So*, without any special explanations, let me disappear behind the opening curtain of this book.

Translated from the Hungarian by John Bátki.

The Smell of Humans

Let's Get Up

On 20 October 1944, which was the sixth day of the Szálasi regime,* at five-thirty (in the morning) Mr T., our 'apartment commander', jolted me from the sweetest of dreams.

'Get up. You have to get up.'

I can't say I was overjoyed by this wake-up call; the night before I had read, as usual, until one or one-thirty. By the time I raised myself on my elbows my two sisters were already standing by my bed, actually sofa, smiling at me.

'Nothing to worry about . . . just another line-up . . . it must be some kind of roll-call . . .'

The apartment commander had already rushed out.

* Szálasi was the head of the extremist Arrow Cross party that seized power during the last months of the war. [All notes have been added by the translator.]

He, too, had to get ready.

There had been a call-up of Jews on 1 October. The army physician, who recognized me, leaned close to examine my eyes for about twenty seconds before diagnosing an inflammation, and threw in a heart condition for good measure. That gave me a three-month deferment, until 1 January. And where would the war be by then?

The 'building commander', Mr K., also knocked on the door: was I up? Sorry, but all gentlemen of Jewish origin must line up downstairs in the vestibule within thirty minutes. We should bring food for two days. I washed from the waist up, my younger brother shaved me (he too was coming); I gulped down a cup of herbal tea and a slice of bread (we were butterless), and swallowed about six plums. My sisters, having packed our rucksacks with whirlwind speed, now strapped mine on my shoulders, and placed a walking cane and a light blanket over my arm.

There were already about thirty-five 'yellow stars' in the lobby,* men standing around in a vague formation facing the entrance, all loaded up, some with enormous, many-pocketed backpacks, plus four or five little parcels and boxes dangling from their hands. Most of the gentlemen were between 50 and 60 years old, a few under 50; some as old as 65, 70, 72 even. Upstairs, the building commander had made it clear that there was no age limit, we all had to go. I stepped into the line next to Mr B., a dear man, company director in civilian life. Each minute brought more yellow-starred tenants packed to go. A black-shirted lad who looked about seventeen stood with his back to the entrance. Bareheaded, without waistcoat or jacket, he wore the black shirt and Arrow Cross armband, and had a holster on his brand-new, yellow leather belt. His

* Hungarian Jews were required to wear yellow stars after the German occupation in March 1944.

hands clutched one of those repulsive, big old rifles, the butt resting between his boots. Bayonet fixed, ready to charge. That lad stood stock still, eyeing us in a decidedly unfriendly manner. The gate was locked. A policeman, also young, armed with rifle and revolver, stood by the wall near the list of tenants' names. Up above the courtyard, behind the guard-rails lining the galleries of all six floors, women and children were watching us. They were not allowed to come down. The building commander and the deputy building commander, Baron D., (both of them Gentiles) were coming and going on small errands: one of the yellow stars had left his cigarettes upstairs, another his razor, yet another his medication. Here came a late arrival gingerly descending the stairs: an elderly gentleman who directed an enquiring glance and an upward toss of the head at a friend facing his way – the kind of look that accompanies the question: 'What do you say to this, old man?'

Baron D. had already whispered in my ear the news that four other Arrow Cross youths were combing the upper floors to make sure no one was trying to hide. Yes, here came another lagging yellow-starred tenant, and another. That made about fifty of us. Some conversed in whispers but most were looking down at their feet in silence.

Well, at last just about all of us were together. The clock on the wall showed six-twenty. Down the stairs came the four youths outfitted with armbands, bayonets and revolvers, with the concierge in tow. Two went down with him to the bomb shelter, the other two took the elevator to the roof terrace. Only two bedridden invalids, too sick to move, were allowed to stay upstairs. All of a sudden the lad standing guard by the entrance bellowed at someone:

'Take off those gloves!'

At the head of the line one of the gentlemen had apparently taken the liberty of putting on his gloves, because the

thin strings of his packages were cutting into his fingers. He
started to explain this in a gentle, patient voice, but the young-
ster screamed at him again:

'Shut up!'

A loud silence ensued. I could hear a sigh behind my
back.

That boy was quite handsome; he wore his long hair
slickly plastered down. In civilian life he could have passed for
an art student. I think he must have worked in a factory; he
was probably someone who yelled himself hoarse at a soccer
game. Perhaps he was not a bad fellow, and it was only the
revolver, the bayonet, and the ideology, of course, that had
turned him into a wild beast.

He cocked his head high, and roared at us:

'Fall in by fours, at the double!'

This was accomplished after some slight confusion;
naturally some of the gentlemen preferred to stand next to a
friend. It took five or six minutes for the shuffling on the
ceramic tiles to cease, until we stood there in good order. There
we stood, and ten, twenty minutes went by. We were not
allowed to smoke, get a drink of water, lean against something
or lie down. Talking was also forbidden. Now it was past seven.
What about that draft? And when were we going? The gentlemen hung their heads in sad, sad thought. About the sons and
in-laws away in forced labour, whom they had not seen for
years, and had not even received any letters from, lately.
About married daughters far from the capital, or aged parents
in the countryside, all of whom had been deported that summer, taken to Germany. In my anxiety I kept shrugging my
shoulders, first the left then the right; the straps were tight,
those two straps of the rucksack. I saw the others doing the
same, shrugging and jerking their shoulders, raising their
hands to contemplate them, like actors in a stage drama. Or

else picking at the fingernails of the left hand, using the right thumbnail, out of sheer boredom. A gentleman who had a tic now twitched his head back even more frequently than usual; after each head-jerk his mouth gaped open three times, so urgently that you'd think he was trying to swallow flies. Another gentleman, without any hand luggage, studied his wedding ring, twisting and turning it. Another kept rubbing the right side of his face with the back of his hand, rubbing, rubbing, like a man who'd just shaved, only he'd been doing this, with brief pauses, for the past fifteen minutes. Three ranks ahead of me someone, with exquisite patience, was scraping away at a spot on his coat sleeve. Up above, by the guard-rail on the third floor, a woman, who had started to wipe away her tears, turned around and went inside.

Two youths came down the stairs wearing army uniforms with armbands. One of them (a corporal) stopped on the lowest step to survey our gathering and issued the command:

'Fall in by threes!'

After much stamping and shuffling of feet we stood lined up by threes. Moving back from my row was Dr A., a chemical engineer who had worked for twenty-five years in a laboratory in Paris. He came home about fifteen years ago. He and his wife were so tormented by homesickness, they just had to come back home.

The corporal called out to the guard at the entrance:

'Szabó and Trajcsik still in the cellar?'

'Yes.'

'What the hell is taking them so long?'

Now the two soldiers went after Szabó and Trajcsik, down into the air-raid shelter. Meanwhile we were kept standing there. They were gone for another quarter of an hour, in no hurry to come back at all. We stood and stood. We stood and stood and stood. In the army, back in the First War, this was how we had to stand around in the courtyard of the barracks, waiting for orders. We stood waiting, waiting, waiting, wasting the precious moments of our youth, nearly going mad with boredom and impatience. This is how the military prepares you, this is how the army makes an obedient corpse out of you. A fly lands on your hand, or your nose itches – what a stroke of luck! At least it gives you something to do, a moment's diversion. Outside, the men, women and children passing by our building would stop for a quick look at our yellow-star troop; we, too, allowed our eyes to trail after anyone going past. When someone coughed, ten, twenty coughs followed suit, just like in the theatre; lucky lungs, someone had thought of them. Men of a certain age, smokers, hack and hawk like this, mornings, for a good five or ten minutes. A few now succumbed to the coughing attack that usually follows the first cigarette of the day. They shook their heads ruefully, made all sorts of efforts to repress the rising cough; most couldn't even reach for a handkerchief because their hands were full of packages. The ensuing silence was broken only by the streetcar's clatter or the rumble of an occasional car. There was a war going on in the world, dear God; and war was a raging madness, isn't that so? And yet the world could be so peaceful and still, so replete with slowly dragging time and boredom. I had never, never lived through such monotonous, still-born hours as on the Serbian front in 1914, during lulls when no shrapnel was bursting overhead. What in holy hell's name could those four warriors be doing down in the cellar for so long? My neighbour on the left, Mr B., the director, whispered his mounting concern about the safety of his air-raid shelter kit. He, too, kept all those most precious items we like to stuff into our air-raid bags down there. There was a shelf set aside for them in a corner of the shelter.

At last the four soldiers emerged into daylight. The last

two were also very young, barely twenty. The corporal looked us over, and pronounced the command:

'I want a head count. There should be 54 men.'

Two soldiers leaped up and ran to the entrance, where one of them started to count by turning sideways and slashing the air with his arm, and taking a step back with each slash:

'Three, six, nine . . .'

The other, as if to check the count, followed in his footsteps. All 54 were present and accounted for.

The corporal:

'*Atten-shun!*'

We stood at attention, like little cub scouts. Next to me Mr B., the director, could not suppress a smile, and I likewise; fortunately our smiles went unnoticed. The boy with the slicked-down hair opened the door. Again, the corporal spoke up: it was like a loudspeaker reverberating in the vestibule of our six-storey building, in the middle of which rose the spiral staircase, a modern design.

'Listen up: we march in total silence and order. No talking. Keep even intervals. If you lag behind or step out of line you'll get a taste of the rifle-butt. Forward march!'

The gentlemen, those who could see the upper floors, sent up cautious, sidelong glances of farewell. We marched out of the building at ten past eight.

The Apartment House on Pozsonyi Road

The door through which we marched out was the front entrance of an apartment house on Pozsonyi Road. My brother, sisters and I had been living there since the end of June, when Jews were ordered by law to move into designated buildings (no doubt to encourage their notorious solidarity). A large, yellow, six-pointed star, the Star of David, was nailed on the front door. On Margaret Island, where I had been living, everyone had to clear out even earlier, on Sunday 19 March, when German troops occupied the country. Two hundred and seventy German officers were billeted at the Hotel Palatinus. I was the only guest permitted to stay until Monday for, unlike the transients, who had a suitcase or two, I was loaded down with books, pictures and all my belongings – my whole life, in fact. I had lived on that island for 33 years. When I set out at eight in the morning, seated on a trunk on top of the horse-drawn wagon, dear old Misley the desk clerk took leave of me and told me not to worry, I would be back in a couple of weeks. This was not a real military occupation, he said; oh no, not at all, it was only a *transitory passage to secure supply lines*. He had this in strict confidence straight from the quartermaster's corps. And I really believed him; it felt so good to believe something. When I passed on the good news in town everyone laughed at me. I moved in with my sisters on Thököly Road. From there we moved in June to the yellow-star building on Pozsonyi Road, to share a fourth-floor apartment, having spent a painful, miserable fortnight waiting around until at the last minute we found bearable accommodations. On moving day we received a foretaste of what was to come: the mover's helpers helped themselves to some of our better items of clothing and linen. Their skill, approaching legerdemain, was such that my two sisters, who supervised the movers, never noticed a thing. And I had even offered cognac to the scoundrels before they set out, as the morning was unusually cool; plus they were given an extra 100 pengős for lugging the upright piano to the fourth floor on Pozsonyi Road.

In that apartment we occupied the maid's diminutive room, and a fine larger room with a balcony facing the Danube. We shared the balcony with our neighbour, Dr László Bakonyi, a most pleasant and cultured man, retired court clerk and son of Samu Bakonyi, secretary-general of the religious community and well-known opposition party deputy from Debrecen. The large apartment also sheltered a third party, a small family of a humbler sort; their part also had a balcony, as well as the bathroom, which of course was shared by all. Dr Bakonyi lived there with his wife, little daughter and 80-year-old mother; she was at the age when some women turn into charming little girls again. I very much enjoyed hearing the savoury Debrecen accents of Mama Bakonyi. Also living with them (sleeping on a trunk in the hall, where she sat or lay down almost all day) was an old nanny. This old nanny was not a blood relative; poor thing, she was a destitute governess, taken in by the Bakonyis ten years before, out of charity. So now we, too, had a chance to experience first-hand some of the not exactly desirable features of living in close quarters with families of strangers. I recalled reading about the life of families sharing an apartment, and even a single room, in Moscow during the first years of the revolution, in Romanov's novel *Three Pairs of Silk Stockings*. But our situation seemed bearable, compared to theirs.

Glass

We moved on a Saturday. And here is what happened the very first night. Around midnight, as I was sleeping off the fatigues of moving day, the air-raid siren started to howl. We roused ourselves and headed for the shelter. We had hardly taken a few steps when there was a tremendous explosion, followed by the sound of glass shattering all over the place. The women were screaming, children bawling, as we all stumbled down the stairs in the dark, sweeping along and tripping over the slower older folks and tottering invalids with their walking canes, sending them wailing and tumbling down the steps, lucky to escape without broken ribs. We were cooped up in the air-raid shelter for about two hours. On our return upstairs, we found our apartment flooded by bright moonlight, for the blinds had been torn off; the parquet floor, the carpets and Torontál kilims were all covered with sparkling bits of shattered glass. The room had a large double picture window along one wall. That window was no more. Tables, chairs, bedspreads, blankets, sheets, pillows and everything else were covered with glistening fragments of glass. The great, big Venetian blinds were all tangled up, pointing every which way in the air, as if there had been a wild party. The partition between the neighbours' section of the apartment and ours had also been made of glass and that too lay on the floor in a myriad fragments. Our pillows and quilts had been slashed through and through by flying slivers of glass. It took us until six-thirty in the morning to pick up and clean away that ocean of broken glass from our beds, floor, tables and chairs. Still, for months afterwards we kept discovering fragments that winked at us from carpets and cracks in the floor. In our building all windows facing the street and all glass partitions were shattered. One bomb landed right in front of the entrance; we couldn't go in or out until all the broken glass and rubble was cleared away. Fortunately this was in the summer, so that the absence of window-panes was bearable. But the lights could not be turned on at night, because we were unable to black out our windows. And so I was not allowed to read at night all summer long, which for me was the worst kind of hardship. (By the end of August, the management had the windows and blinds repaired.) In the course of this summer, on moonless nights I learned to eat my supper in the dark. We ate a cold meal every night; by groping about I was able to find knife, fork, spoon and my food – in short, everything. I even learned to eat noiselessly, for my sisters and our neighbours were all asleep. I rolled my cigarettes in the dark. I think I was born with this gift; back in the Serbian campaign during the First War, marching through wooded hills at night, I showed off for the gentlemen of the regimental staff by rolling factory-perfect cigarettes in pelting rain on horseback, the reins wrapped around my wrist, while my horse kept slipping in the mud. This is about the only military glory I can boast of. To light one up here on Pozsonyi Road after supper, I had to sneak out into the pantry, where no one could see the flame. Deprived of my reading, after eleven-thirty I would pace back and forth on the balcony for an hour and more above the silent, blacked-out city. It was nine steps down the length of the balcony, as long as you didn't take large steps. I have no idea how many times I turned and turned about for those nine steps, in the course of an hour. Margaret Island lay straight ahead in the dark, but I refrained from glancing in that direction, and kept my eyes mostly on the sky and the water, or on the Castle and Gellért Hill across the Danube. For the first few days my heart nearly broke each time I caught a glimpse, from the balcony or through the window, of my beloved island, so green. As I said, I sat down to supper late, around ten; after ten-thirty the ladies and gentlemen of the late-night crowd on our floor would get together at Herr Direktor V.'s, to listen to the ten o'clock Hungarian broadcast from London. In that inner room the light could shine undetected. V., a long-time tenant of this building, happened to be the neighbour and good friend of Baron D., who hailed from Austria and hated the Reich with a passion. And since people of Jewish descent were prohibited by law to own radios, Herr Direktor V. listened to the broadcast at Baron D.'s with paper and pencil in hand to take down the nightly broadcast in shorthand. The Baron could not invite the whole crowd, it would have aroused suspicion. Afterwards, Herr Direktor V. would return to his room and read the transcript for the benefit of the assembled company. This little bit of London each night, I must say, felt very good. After a brief discussion of the latest events, the gentlemen would take their leave around eleven, everyone tiptoeing home with many a whispered goodnight.

The Air-Raid Shelter

I got acquainted with some of my fellow tenants in the air-raid shelter, where we found ourselves four or five times on some days. At first I tried to stay in the apartment, but the building commander always sent up for me, and I had to go down. By now here at home we had become inured to what we had read about with such horror earlier in the war, at the time of the bombing of Antwerp. When I tried to hide upstairs in the apartment during an air raid, and a bomb exploded nearby, I was frightened for a moment but went on reading nonetheless. For us Jews the worst tribulation was our defencelessness, and our chief fear, deportation to a concentration camp. Death in a bomb explosion was no big deal, in comparison. As at our former address on Thököly Road, here too during air raids I would go up for a cigarette break in the courtyard. On Pozsonyi Road we had quite a group of smokers – men and women who would have stayed in the courtyard for the duration of the air raid, had the building commander not chased us downstairs in the thick of the explosions. He himself wouldn't have minded our freedom, but feared the block commander, who had a penchant for turning up during air raids; anyone found upstairs was in for severe penalties. So we were cooped up in that shelter for four or five hours at a time. Our air-raid shelter was a fine, large, whitewashed basement divided into two halves with room for about four hundred people. It was fairly decently lit at night, but the bulbs were high up on the ceiling; reading on the bench was too tiring for my eyes. There were always two or three chess games in progress, just like good old peacetime, and one or two klatsches of ladies who passed the tedium of these aerial visitations by playing rummy. Most of the women would knit, or else they brought down potatoes to peel, green beans and peas to shell. And then of course there were those who did not fuss with anything but kept up a steady stream of chatter. There was a type, including both men and women, who would always be nibbling at something, night and day. Once or twice the bombs struck so close that the ground trembled under our feet and the lights went out. Screaming women would jump up in the dark, and babies bawled. Little girls would help out their mothers with a squeal or two. But otherwise the children had a great time whenever the alarm sounded. Little boys and girls were past masters at imitating the siren; they loved flares and the red tracers at night, it was fairy-tale stuff. The kitties not only walked about undeterred during bombing raids but actually frolicked. It is interesting to note that dogs, a species closer to the human in character, were, for the most, restless, trembling and whimpering while those murderous bombs flailed Budapest. Could it be because they are more loyal and fear for their masters? All the little boys in our building had their own miniature civil defence armbands and belts complete with toy axe. One or two even had their own ash-grey civil defence helmets. Some of our civil defence officers resembled these children at their games; we had four or five of them who peered out from under their helmets, living in a veritable military fantasy. These characters marched ramrod straight with stiff steps along the cellar walls, pulling their rope belts tight, fingering their axes or fidgeting with those grim helmets; baleful, unsmiling faces forever reprimanding the rambunctious children to be quiet.

It was touching to see how, nearly every day, Mama Bakonyi was carried to the shelter by her son, Dr László Bakonyi, himself of frail physique. (Poor man, worn away by the forced labour of digging fortifications and the subsequent food shortage in the ghetto, died of starvation in March, at the age of fifty.) The Bakonyis' 10-year-old Katie had a passion for civil defence. She would run home exultant from one of her girl-friends, and shout across the blankets and sheets separating the two halves of the apartment:

'Yikes, intruder aircraft over Budapest!' She jumped for joy, not out of fright. Katie was happy, she truly was; she grabbed whatever she had to carry and was the first in the cellar, where she was the ringleader in the children's games. At times she would shout across the partition: 'Uncle Ernő, intruder aircraft at Pécs and Eger! BUDAPEST IS NEXT!'

But it would be a false alarm. So we named her 'Airraid Katie'.

The siren had the annoying habit of screaming out at the precise instant each morning when you were about to take that first swallow of tea, or strike the match to light up, or stood there with half your face shaved, or were in some even more embarrassing spot. It was really hard to excuse such rudeness.

T.

One after another I got to know the gentlemen in the building. Across from us on our landing lived Mr T., director of a shipping, excuse me, transportation company, one of the original tenants of this apartment house. Living with him were his daughter-in-law (ever since his son had been taken for forced labour in the Ukraine) and his grandson, as well as his daughter-in-law's mother and younger sister. This way he did not have to accommodate any strangers in his apartment. Mr T. was a highly educated, much-travelled gentleman with a distinguished bearing, whose rich library furnished me with abundant reading matter as long as we were left in peace. I had another source of books on our floor in the person of Mr V., another company director and long-time tenant, who provided many an English and French volume, classics that I had been meaning to read for some time. As for my own English-language books, earlier that spring I had left the hardback volumes in the care of a friend whose religious background was more auspicious than mine; the paperback Tauchnitz, Albatross and Penguin editions I burned, after a visiting writer friend of mine gave me a great scare. He said that any Jew found possessing English-language books would be deported; as a Jewish writer I should be aware that I was under observation. So my sisters and I used these English books and some problematic Hungarian texts we owned to heat the bathroom for ten days running. It was a cold spring and firewood and coal were rare commodities.

Day by day I got to like Mr T. more and more. He taught me something new. He introduced me to a realm I hadn't known existed: the realm of transportation. This vast realm includes the five continents and the seven seas. Mr T. had business contacts in India and Sudan, Japan and the Cape of Good Hope; he was able to ship, excuse me, transport anything from anywhere to any place. He had a shelf full of encyclopedic volumes, each page containing international transportation maps, published in England. We spent entire mornings studying these marvellously detailed maps; maps of Russian, French, Italian provinces, depending on the volume. After breakfast I always dropped in on Mr T. and recapitulated the London broadcast of the night before. (He went to bed early.) By then we would have the morning papers as well. Mr T., using a compass, measured the distances on the map and calculated how many days to Königsberg and Livorno, how many weeks till we reach Paris. He was my military attaché. Oh, how I missed him when he was conscripted for rubble clean-up. He was gone from six in the morning to six at night for about three weeks, until he had the good fortune of an iron post falling on his foot. After that he and his swollen foot were confined to the sofa. What pained him, in addition to his foot, was that he could no longer cart rubble in a wheelbarrow, for, after all, it was something to do. The gentlemen in this building complained bitterly about the trials of their enforced idleness. Some of them, forced into retirement or fired outright as a result of anti-Jewish decrees, had not worked for five or six years. All of these once-active men in our building could testify that there is nothing more tiring than inactivity. We had an architect who kept designing temples, museums, crematoria, just to keep from going crazy.

For me too, not being able to work was a severe hardship. When we were forced to relocate I stopped working on my novel in progress; under these circumstances I could not and dared not work. I could be searched; and whatever I wrote would be considered traitorous. All I could do was make entries in a pocket notebook; whenever the doorbell rang I hid it in a pillowcase. Oh, the terror of the ringing doorbell! You never knew if it wasn't someone with evil intentions, come to take away the Jews.

Or the great scares when someone who had gone out wasn't back by five in the afternoon! (We were permitted to go out on the street from 3 to 5 p.m.) A few minutes after five everyone had to be out in front of their door on the corridor, waiting for the building commander to come and take a headcount to make sure all persons whose names were on the door were present. This task was assigned to Baron D., who was both embarrassed and annoyed by it. After a week, it was left up to the apartment commander to check if everyone was back or not. After another two weeks, he too gave up on it. After that, it was up to us to notify the house commander about any family member not home by five. He in turn was under strictest orders to report at the police station by six.

As for me, I never went out; I did not feel like walking around with a yellow star. Every two weeks I went across the street to the barber's for a haircut and a session with the manicure lady. Back in April, when we had to sew on those yellow stars, I thought I would die, degraded to the level of a branded beast, a marked object. No, they wouldn't see me wearing that star. Back on Thököly Road I had the barber and the manicure girl come over to the apartment; I did not set foot on the street. That house had a garden at the back, where I could walk for an hour in the morning and at night. Inside the fence one did not have to wear the yellow star. Until we had to move again I never wore the coat with the star sewn on it. At the end of June I had to go out (wearing that star) to the Jewish community office, to find an apartment. I pulled my hat over my eyes, ostrich-like. On the streetcar I could feel my face getting red-hot with shame. Here on Pozsonyi Road we had to wear the star even on the staircase. The anti-Jewish decrees had finely nuanced provisions against Jews living in the same building visiting each other. For a few days we obeyed, until Baron D. let it be understood that we were to visit as we pleased and he hoped there wouldn't be any trouble.

My Days

If you are not bored by all this, dear reader, I would like to tell you how I spent my days. I hope you won't mind. As I said, my mornings, from ten to eleven, were spent in the company of Mr T. After that I would read till one or one-thirty. From time to time I scribbled in my notebook ideas for future immortal works. We had lunch after two, although some days it would be at four or even five, after a lengthy air raid, or if my sister could not find anything at the store or market during the noontime leave (lasting from eleven to two). If there was no disturbance, I would sit on the balcony and watch the passing barges and clouds.* I used to be able to play the piano, but not

---

* Clouds constitute one of the favourite themes of Ernő Szép's poetry.

once did I try here on Pozsonyi Road. Neither did my sisters. Not one of the piano players in that building dared to make music, or had the heart to play. Women whose husbands, brothers and sons were clearing minefields on the Russian front, how could they play a dreamy Debussy theme while their loved ones might be torn apart by an explosion, or tied up and beaten to death?

After lunch I would pace for an hour or so on the balcony. Then I would read until about six, when I went to visit Herr Direktor V., the gentleman who reported on the London broadcast. His son had been taken away, and they had no news of him. We never talked about the boy; his parents were unable to bring him up without rending each other's heart. The boy wrote poems; as a university student all he ever wanted to be was a poet. Now even that would have been acceptable for the parents, if only their son could come home. They were good people; they had taken in more relatives than the number of people designated for the size of the apartment. Women of all ages and their children. The beautiful, big apartment was full of beds, armchairs and sofa beds. They did all the shopping, house-cleaning, washing; Jews were forbidden by law to employ a maid. Actual Jews, that is officially of the Israelite denomination, were hard to find among the tenants of this yellow-starred house. It was mostly Catholics and Protestants; but their parents and grandparents . . . I would stay for an hour at Herr Direktor V.'s, even though he wasn't home some days, when he went to play bridge at a neighbour's. There were several bridge parties going on in the long afternoon hours, as well as games of rummy; the older gentlemen played only the old-fashioned game with traditional Hungarian cards.

Anti-Semitic Jews

Visiting the neighbours was much in vogue; naturally each to his own. Choices were made not only along economic lines or social tone, oh no: there were anti-Semitic bigots (born Christians or converts of twenty years' standing) who would have nothing to do with Jews – that is, those Christians who had converted recently. They wouldn't even allow their children to play with those of recent converts. At the Thököly Road air-raid shelter a woman of German-Hungarian extraction, a postal employee, would not sit next to my sister, a teacher of Hungarian. Here on Pozsonyi Road, during our first visit to the shelter, we were treated to the following edifying incident. One lady jumped up from her seat, shouting: 'I'm not sitting next to that Jew!' The other lady, who had sat there with her husband, turned towards us plaintively: 'What can you say to that kind of cheek? We have been Catholics for over two years.'

Both women wore diamond crosses on a chain. Converted women were often more anti-Semitic than their husbands. But almost every Jew, even those who stayed in their denomination, was an anti-Semite, revolted by the other Jews. For he was made to suffer because of 'their sins'. Oh, if he were the only Jew in the world, he would be revered like a holy relic! But there were too many Jews in the world. If there weren't any, then he wouldn't have been born a Jew either.

I chatted with the charming, bright women at Herr Direktor V.'s. There were some very good-looking women here and there in the house; you might ask, did I try courting one or another. The answer is no; even though I was as starved for love as for a cigarette. But no, no and no, I did not have the gall, the heart and soul to make up to a woman whose man had been carried away. There is no flirtation or affair that is purely a matter of the senses. Nor can I say of any woman in the building that she offered herself in words or by any other sign to me or any other man around. Although they lived in daily sorrow and fear, as women they still cared about their looks, and applied powder and lipstick with feline fastidiousness. Females have a way of smiling or a vigilant glance that asks every day, do you like to look at me, do you find me desirable? They seem to need that as much as a breath of air.

F.

Around six-thirty I usually had my tea, and bread and butter (when we had butter), or else some cherries or sourcherries. My sisters had their dinner around my teatime. Then they set out my dinner on the coffee table by the unglazed window. After tea I read for a while before going out on the third of my regular visits, down to the F. apartment on the first floor. Mr F. was an engineer, around forty, tall and handsome; he could have passed for one of those fabled Debrecen hussar officers of yore. At the age of 28, working on the floodgates of the Körös River, Mr F. happened to notice some old peasant women gathering herbs in the field. They sold their harvest to the local apothecary. A year later, paying the poor villagers ten times the going rate, he was marketing the herbs of that region nationwide. Two years later his small company was selling the herbs all over Europe; by the third year he was distributing the herbal blessing from the banks of the Körös as far away as America. He was invited there to manage a large herbal firm, where he introduced many of these plants from Hungary. In 1939 he came home to visit his aged mother, and remained stranded here. He claims that if the war hadn't broken out, by now he would be marketing Hungarian herbs in North and South America. (Does this sound like an 'enemy of the homeland'?) Besides marketing and management, Mr F.'s chief mission was the improvement of plant species. And here he was now confined to languish inactive in this building, with his mother and sister whose husband had been taken away.

It was interesting that this most modern young man followed to the letter the most orthodox Jewish laws, along the lines of the religious education he had received. The F. family was strictly kosher. Friday nights Mama F. lit the candles, her daughter by her side, praying with closed eyes and clasped hands in front of two burning candles. These burned until blackout time, when someone came from the neighbouring Gentile apartment to blow them out. For orthodox Jews are not allowed to blow out a candle after the onset of the Sabbath. Mr F. told me something amusing: no matter where he travelled, he was able to find kosher restaurants, thanks to an orthodox Jewish Baedeker that listed just about every ritually pure restaurant in the world. (I too recalled a Friday night dinner with Lajos Bíró at a Jewish bistro in the Quartier Latin, where we sampled a famous pike dish. The *patron*, wearing a beret, swore blind that even his Bordeaux wine was bona fide kosher.) Naturally Mr F. always had his head covered when eating. But what really impressed me was that from the lighting of the candles Friday evening until the end of the Sabbath Saturday night he would never smoke, even though he was a passionate cigar smoker. Hats off to him, and I hope Jehovah does not take amiss my uncovered head.

Mr F., being only forty, had been exempted from forced

labour because a car accident a few years earlier had fractured his vertebrae. He had to wear a tight surgical corset at all times.

Almost every evening at Mr F.'s a young cousin of his, in his early twenties, came to visit. This young man worked at some factory and wore a white armband; Jewish forced labourers who were converted Christians wore white instead of yellow. This boy did not look Jewish at all, and, passing for a Christian, he was able to sneak away each night without getting caught. He wore a Hungarian soldier's cap, as did all forced labourers with or without yellow armbands. There were other young men who visited the house, forced labourers playing hooky, sneaking in from the outskirts of town. None of them had typical Jewish looks, and of course they took off their white or yellow armbands for the trip. These daring fellows visited their parents, relatives or sweethearts.

F.'s guest would have been a law student, if it hadn't been for the war. Each day he brought news, and good news at that. First off he reported on the five o'clock London broadcast. They were always able to get the latest from London, because his lieutenant allowed the Jews assigned to work in his office to listen along with him. This lieutenant was a decent sort, and bright; he had known from the beginning that the Germans wouldn't last nine rounds. He addressed the Jewish forced labourers as 'Mister', and apologized daily for having to work them so hard. But even among the lower ranks of the guards there were some who hated the Germans, especially since they had occupied the country. On this day there had been another incident, when two German officers insisted on passing through the gate to check on the Jews loading the wagons. The Hungarian soldiers refused to admit them, and when the two Germans pulled guns, they knocked these out of their hands and chased them away with rifle-butts. Next he told us the latest news heard on the streetcar: the Russians had reached Warsaw. At the front lines there seemed to be an increasing number of clashes between the Hungarian and German troops. After all of this he could have his well-earned coffee with cake, butter and cigarettes. Later, Mr F. would play a game of chess with Mr T., who came by in the evenings; the two were devoted chess players.

Next, between eight and nine, I dropped in on my neighbour, Dr Bakonyi, who always came home late from the Jewish Community office, where workers were granted freedom of movement from eight to eight. Dr Bakonyi usually walked home. He found it painful to sit in the back of the streetcar, in the car designated for Jews. Also the walk helped clear his aching head; each day his office was besieged during the hours of free passage by hundreds of Jews with their thousands of problems. Dr Bakonyi was the office liaison with the Ministry regarding Jewish affairs. He too was full of news each day, but this wasn't very good news. The previous day he had had something heartening to relate: Governor Horthy had managed to prevent the deportation to Germany of 1,500 Jews, mostly socialists, lawyers and members of the press corps, who had already been loaded into freight trains at Kistarcsa station . . . But tonight he called me out to the balcony to let me know that one of his Ministry contacts had informed him about impending trouble: 3,000 gendarmes had been called up to Budapest. This was again the work of the Germans, who wanted to liquidate the Jews of Budapest. He had not said a word about this to his wife and mother. You can imagine how I slept that night. I trembled for my frail sisters, who would never survive deportation to Germany. And I feared for my dear friends and acquaintances and for everyone, one and all. I was well aware that many Jews were carrying cyanide on their persons, in case of deportation. My sisters and brother had not taken this precaution. Late in the summer, by the time my sisters started to talk about it, the poison was impossible to come by. Then we dropped the idea, and Dr Bakonyi encouraged us by saying that the Jews of the capital were safe from further disasters. It is hard to tell you how I felt about this, with regard to my own person. I had given poison a moment's thought, once or twice. But it was as if I couldn't believe in death. Oh yes, I too would eventually be snuffed out like a candle, but I would no longer be there to know about it. I don't know, I don't believe, I cannot imagine anything other than life. There will never be an end to life; after the last breath, I will not put away my lungs; after the last thought I will not place a full stop: breath and thought will leap into the infinite, the timeless. I am deathless; that is, unable to die. We all are. And I am so curious, so very curious about everything on Earth; so madly desirous of seeing, hearing, knowing the whole world and all of life, that I would even attend my own hanging with curiosity. I would not swallow poison even to avoid being tossed into the gas chamber.

The Entrance

I forgot to tell you about the night watch. Early in July the tenants got together, along with the people in the neighbouring yellow-star houses, to organize a night watch. There was talk of patrols entering yellow-star buildings to extort and rob from the tenants. From then on we kept our front entrance locked at all times, with two men guarding it in two-hour shifts night and day. It was my turn for night watch two nights a week; my shift was never set later than midnight. The plan was this: in case one of these patrols wanted to force entry (the janitor wasn't going to let them in), the night watch would cross from our roof to the neighbouring building that had an exit on Rakovszky Park. One would run to the nearby police station, the other to the nearest army barracks for help. There was a small box for the night watch outside the janitor's apartment in the vestibule, with the guard duty-list posted on the wall. If some dull oldster was assigned to be my mate, the kind Mr T. came downstairs to help me pass those two hours. The guard box accommodated a small table and two chairs; the janitor let us borrow his radio so we could listen to music as long as we kept the volume down. But most of the time it was dance music and the caterwauling of some pop star, which we turned off. Alas, there was no reading in there, with only a tiny blue bulb for light.

Our two decent building commanders, Mr K. and Baron D., condoned the yellow-star tenants sunning themselves on the roof terrace. (The building had a total of five Gentile apartments.) You can imagine what a blessing this was; lounge chairs from balconies appeared on the roof, and red-and-green-striped beach umbrellas. Bathing suits were taken out of storage; there was even a shower up there, just like at the beach. So the ladies and gentlemen read and played cards on the roof in the afternoons; women who were not card players or slaves to some novel would gossip or do embroidery on the lounge chairs or lying about on the clean 'crazy pavement'.* The uproar of rollicking children always created a problem; little ones just can't take anti-Semitism seriously. It was next to impossible to put a silencer on their laughter and squeals as they romped on the roof. But the eight- and ten-

---

* In English in the original.

year-olds were a sad sight, silent and solemn, sitting off in a corner by themselves, staring at the ground. They knew everything. But we were always afraid on account of the little ones. Someone in the neighbourhood could denounce this Jewish summer holiday, God forbid.

The House Next Door

The second time I went up to the roof I noticed a painter I knew, standing on the roof of the neighbouring building, in front of a landscape in progress. He was painting a corner of the beautiful, verdant island in the Danube. His building was also marked by a yellow star. All I had to do was climb over the waist-high railing separating the two roof terraces. There was another familiar gentleman lying there on his terrycloth robe, brown as a Bedouin.

'Not too bad, eh Maestro?' he said, raising his head. 'Is there a piece of wood here to knock on?'

The painter offered his brush.

With a view of the Danube bridges in front of us my painter friend entertained me with tales of the human condition in his building. In the apartment where he was holed up, his neighbour's mother-in-law was a dotty old lady who was convinced her daughter and son-in-law were trying to poison her. When her grandson brought her breakfast tea, he had to taste it before she drank any; the same for the buttered roll, and even the fruit. When the alarm sounded, they had to practically shove her downstairs (she was rather deaf, by the way); nor would she believe that there was an air raid going on – she imagined her daughter invented it all to terrorize her.

Another woman invalid, one floor higher, was also an interesting case. All day she sat in a wheelchair, paralyzed. She was a Christian, her husband a Jew. The disease had attacked her joints in her youth, and her husband married her nonetheless. (Nor had she been a rich catch.) Well, now that it was so fashionable, this woman too had turned into a rabid anti-Semite. She was a fanatical believer in Hitler, praising the Führer day and night, cussing out the Jews in the meantime. Her two sons had been taken for forced labour, and she had no pity on them. What did I think of her?

Then there was another family: the parents had opposed their daughter's marriage to a penniless young man. But she went ahead and married him. After the forced relocation, the young couple came to live with the parents. After a few days' truce, the ugly scenes started in: right now they were refusing to feed the son-in-law. Whereupon the daughter went on a hunger strike; she cried night and day and wanted to jump out of the window. Then she gave up and started to eat again, but she was not allowed to share her food with her husband, who was fed by the neighbours. The young couple would have moved out, but had no place to go.

And listen to the grotesque situation in a fourth apartment, belonging to a recently divorced woman who lived there with her little daughter. Her boyfriend had moved in, with intentions to marry her. Then she took in two of her women friends and their families. Finally came the divorced husband who could not find a decent place to stay, and took the maid's room in that big apartment. They said the divorced husband was head over heels in love with his ex-wife. A ready-made novel, wouldn't you say?

Oh, how many apartments in how many buildings contained such raging infernos? It was enough to make you think of Mauriac, or Céline.

Petition the Governor

The days passed as usual: Monday, Tuesday, Wednesday – not even the kind of world we lived in during those days could break up the order of their sequence. One day around the middle of July Dr Bakonyi brought a message for me from Councillor N. at the Ministry, urging me to petition the Governor for exemption from having to wear the yellow star. Some new policy was supposedly in the making that would remove this onus from noted scientists, writers and artists. According to the Councillor I would be among the very first allowed to remove the star that had been sewn on my overcoat. I was certain that it was Dr Bakonyi who recommended my name to the Councillor's attention. He, Dr Bakonyi, had already been exempted ten days ago, to facilitate his access to the Ministry. You may imagine how shameful I found this: making sure to include in the petition a statement that I had never done anything against the nation. No, you couldn't have fathomed the shame of one who had been called to rise above his nation by the very nature of his vocation as writer – now forced to beg to be considered just as much a part of the Hungarian nation as any dog catcher or criminal under lock and key. And why should I be treated differently from my fellow sufferers marked by yellow stars? But getting rid of the yellow star would have meant that my sisters could go to the market earlier so that we, who were short of money, could buy our food at regular prices, instead of the black-market rates demanded by pedlars who came to the house after hours to offer exorbitantly expensive meat, sugar, butter, potatoes, green beans and fruit. We were losing weight at a rapid rate. Meanwhile the prospect of deportation and certain death hung over our heads . . . The exempted ones could not be taken away. As I said earlier, I myself had no fear of perishing. I could have sworn that we would survive. Perhaps only the weak, such as myself, can have such insanely strong beliefs. But I had a heavy burden of responsibility: my brother and sisters. So the next day we wrote that petition. I kept having visual hallucinations: my lines turned red with shame, as if I were using red ink. Dr Bakonyi conveyed the petition to the Ministry. I tried to allay my shame by resolving not to flaunt this starless freedom, not to go out on the street, just as before. I also resolved to keep on wearing the star at home in our building, so as not to make the humiliation of the others any worse, not to give them cause for envy.

I can't recall so well all the things that happened that summer. My mind is still exhausted, and besides, I seem to have a considerable talent for rapidly forgetting historical events. I no longer recall when Sztójay went, and when Lakatos was appointed Prime Minister in his stead. Perhaps back in July. It was all the same; for us what mattered most was that 3,000 gendarmes with rooster feathers on their hats had been called up to Budapest. Dr Bakonyi brought us news of a dozen policemen holding the line against the multitudes besieging his office, seeking passage to Palestine. The Russians still had not reached our borders, and were dawdling at the Transylvanian mountain passes. Who could tell when we would be liberated, if at all. The whole building was debating who this Lakatos was and what could be expected of him. The consensus had it that he was a professional soldier loyal to Governor Horthy. But there was little he could do, while the Germans were occupying the country.

Swedish Protection

Around that time we first heard of the Swedish protective passes. Again, Dr Bakonyi was my source. The Swedish
Legation in Budapest would consider as a Swedish citizen and
accordingly transport to Sweden any Jew (or Gentile) with a
relative residing in Sweden.* The only condition was that the
relative in Sweden had to state in writing that he would pay
for the cost of travel and would act as a sponsor for the individ-
ual arriving in Sweden. While waiting here for transport this
lucky person would receive a letter of protection which would
mean the removal of the yellow star and safety from harass-
ment. In our building there were two people with close relations – uncle, brother-in-law – living in Sweden. These two
were now the object of general envy. Of course they immediately wrote letters to Sweden and rushed to deliver these at the
Legation, from where they would be forwarded.

More will follow about this Swedishness; as we all know,
soon it became a flood, a veritable River Tisza bursting its
floodgates.

I have just remembered that during these days I had a
visit from a dear man, Ákos Molnár. He too had received the
Jewish fate as his terrestrial lot. He was a writer and I had
read several of his fine stories; I knew he had written one or
two novels as well, but had not read these. I had met him
once before. Ákos Molnár had only his left arm to write with;
his right arm had been severed by shrapnel in the First War
(which, since 1939, we had been nostalgically referring to
as the 'Peacetime War'). Originally he had started out as a

---

* After the March 1944 German takeover of Hungary the
Swedish Embassy in Budapest was downgraded to a legation as a sign of
non-recognition.

concert violinist; I had heard it said at the Music Academy that his professors predicted a brilliant future for him. But after that thoughtful shrapnel carried off his right arm he had to earn his living at an office job. And he started to write. As he put it, writing was his way of finding consolation. Well, after ferreting out my new address, he looked me up to offer his help in procuring provisions. He had total freedom of movement and no yellow star, on account of being classified 75 per cent disabled. For openers he unloaded two pounds of sugar and one hundred Memphis cigarettes from his briefcase. At uninflated prices. After that he would bring us sugar, butter, honey, tobacco – whatever was available through his usual reliable sources. On his first visit he also had some news about the Governor's exemptions, and followed up on this by visiting several people on my behalf to speed up the process. It turned out that my petition went from the Ministry of Culture to the Prime Minister's office, to be forwarded to Governor Horthy. (Poor Ákos Molnár and his lovely, delicate wife were murdered in December by Arrow Cross youths.)

Within a few days of first hearing about the Swedish protective passes, the whole neighbourhood was off and running to the Swedish Legation. In the meantime the protection was extended to anyone with friends or business partners in Sweden. Mr T., director of the transportation firm, was able to secure protective passes for at least a dozen tenants, through his several business contacts in Sweden. These humanitarian Swedes wrote letters sponsoring their newly assumed 'business associates'. Mr T. himself did not partake of the Swedish help. He was a self-admitted fatalist; it was not his style to accept outside aid. And anyway, he firmly believed that Germany would collapse by September. We could certainly hold out until then. There weren't enough cattle wagons to take away the Jews. In fact he predicted that in a few weeks the

Wehrmacht would turn its arms against the SS; their conflicts were common knowledge. (He said this pointing his index fingers at each other.) I had seen the same gesture from other gentlemen, in the same reference. Then again, we could count on Hungary's jumping the Axis ship before long. How nice it would be if we did it before Romania. I had to admire Mr T. for faithfully keeping to the dictates of his religion, just like Mr F. He prayed each and every morning, refrained from smoking on the Sabbath, attended services and lit the candles on Friday night. Only in the observance of kashrut did he allow himself some leeway. He defended his religious observances by saying that one should take the community seriously. And it was proper to believe in God; we needed God. And he could only keep his belief in God by observing the traditions of his religion, just like his father and grandfather before him. This way he would always remain a reverent child. (Later in the autumn Mr T. was deported to Germany, where this wonderful, kind man perished.)

I remember 20 July very vividly. (The day of the bomb attempt against Hitler.) The whole apartment house, Jews and Gentiles, was in extasy; everyone thought that peace was a mere 48 hours away. That night the London broadcast claimed that Germany was in a state of revolt. Even the next day the broadcast spoke of one regiment after another joining the putsch. The great jubilation began to wilt only on the third day. Now we read the list of generals arrested and sentenced to death. We grieved for these Germans; they were our dead as well, our would-be liberators.

So everyone in the building, all of Pozsonyi Road, kept scurrying back to the Swedish Legation. Sheets had to be filled out, passport photos had to be taken. The London broadcasts remained our only source of hope and solace. It was truly a blessing that we had access to these radio broadcasts in our building. And we kept studying the maps of Russia, Italy, France. The Russians were still far away. Mr T. fantasized about the British being able to reach us through Italy: within a few days they would be in Ancona, from where the Dalmatian coast was three hours by sea. They would unite with Tito's forces, and in less than a week's time (according to Mr T.) they would be in Hungary. But most of the distressed Jews did not possess such strategic imagination and could hardly wait for the evening's London broadcast: how much closer were the Russians getting? Oh, if they were here already! As soon as they reached the border the Hungarians would bolt the Axis camp. Perhaps even sooner. So that the moment Herr Direktor V. began to read out his shorthand notes of the broadcast, several people spread out their maps (a nightly ritual), pencils and fingertips following the place-names. Others took notes on slips of paper, to tell their families about the day's developments and to file away as precious relics. His Excellency Mr E. (chief councillor, in finance) was such a fastidious man that he kept interrupting Herr Direktor V.:

'How many villages exactly?'

'A hundred and thirty-seven.' (That is, the number of villages occupied that day in Poland by the Russians.)

Or else:

'Excuse me, could you spell the name of that town they reached today?'

'S-i-e-d-l-c-e.'

'Ah, thank you.'

And again:

'How many casualties, how many dead?'

'Sixty thousand.'

There were one or two gentlemen and ladies who were in a permanent sulk; from the looks they gave Herr Direktor V. it would have appeared they blamed him for the unnaturally slow advance of the Russians, not to mention the British! Still at Angers, still only at Saint-Lô, for how many days now!

'Trouble is, the British soldier is reluctant to die.' (A certain lady came up with this complaint, and not only once. Women are always more cruel.)

At last Herr Direktor V. lost patience with her:

'Madam, I was in the field for 44 months in the last war, always in the front line, and please believe me that not for a single moment did I want to die. No one wants to die. Please refrain from making that reproach against the brave Tommies who are fighting for us. Plenty of them are dying; I wish we could resurrect all those fine young men.'

Her rejoinder was delivered with a lame laugh:

'I did not mean it that way.'

There is a certain type that always finds out about things instantly: for instance, that fine cigars are available at a particular shop. Or that now Switzerland was also issuing safe conduct passes. Where do they find out about these things? People are amazing. It would be preferable to go to Switzerland, as long as we have to go, rather than to Sweden, where one doesn't speak a word of the language. Not even Dr Bakonyi had heard of this Swiss business and already a handful of people from our building had been to the Swiss Legation. This Swiss flurry began in late July or early August. There were one or two Swiss applicants who already had Swedish passes in the works, so that now they were offered two new homelands by fate, and more: three, in case, God willing, they could remain here in Hungary. As far as that domestic exemption went, the Governor's, well, for some reason it failed to materialize. Two weeks after I sent the petition I received a questionnaire in the mail, which had to be filled out with our personal data. After that, nothing. According to Ákos Molnár these forms were now sent to the police to make sure the peti-

tioner was no militant left-winger, and had not been a communist in 1919. There were no exceptions to this procedure.
None. But, day by day, more and more of the Governor's
exemption papers were turning up in the hands of financial
editors, manufacturers, wholesalers, retailers, financiers,
owners of fashion salons and dance instructors. All this was
well and good; after all, everyone should be exempted from the
odium of the yellow star. But why should that yellow stain stay
the longest on the lapels of writers, scientists and artists?

One week the gendarmes were gone, then all 3,000
were back again. A few days later, the 1,500 intellectuals
entrained at Kistarcsa were suddenly taken away to Germany,
after the Governor had seemingly saved them from the claws
of the SS. The Germans accomplished this in the manner of a
putsch: the Jewish Council was ordered up to the Gestapo
headquarters in the Buda Hills and detained there from mid-
day till nightfall (so no one could run and scream at the
Ministry of the Interior); meanwhile the wretched internees
were loaded into cattle wagons and the train carried them out
of the country.

Who knew – we would never know – their ultimate fate.

Our executioners, the SS boys dressed in black, strutted
in our streets free and easy, eyeing the women and the mer-
chandise in shop windows, meanwhile completely ignoring or
simply laughing at us. Some of them were handsome, seemingly clean-cut young men. In general, many of the Germans
looked remarkably like ordinary human beings created in
God's image. At times you could hear two SS men speaking
Hungarian: these were the offspring of Hungarians of German
extraction. They were in seventh heaven now, their fondest
dream on the verge of coming true: Hungary absorbed by the
Reich.

By the middle of August there was still no word from

the Governor's office. I had a message from a friend to go to a certain address to expedite matters. My sister went in my place and found some kind of literary committee piddling around there. They hoped to return the list to the Ministry of Culture in two or three weeks. My sisters were ready to despair of ever being able to buy meat, lard, sugar and everything else at reasonable prices.

The Germans served up another surprise. For months now the Governor had been tussling with the SS about the fate of the Jews of Újpest. The SS wanted to slap them into wagons just like the other Jews from all the other towns and villages in Hungary. Two to three thousand Jews were trembling in Újpest as their fate hung in the balance from day to day, between going or staying. But lately Dr Bakonyi was of the opinion that the SS had given up on them. Well, one night the gendarmes roused up the Újpest Jews, executed the very old and the sick, and took away the rest, shoving them into wagons with their rifle-butts. So they too were taken from their homeland now.

After this, Dr Bakonyi thought we should seek Swedish protection at once.

At last I agreed to go to the Swedish Legation. I took along something to read on the lengthy streetcar ride (Jews were not permitted to take cabs) and hid my face behind the pages of a book. There were also Gentiles riding in the car designated for Jews, and I felt tremendous shame at not being able to tear that yellow mark from my breast. When I got off the streetcar near the Legation, the air-raid siren sounded. I ran to crouch under the fountain's rim near the Gellért Hotel. There were others taking shelter there already. The only reason I mention this was because two young women there recognized me and whispered my humble name loud enough to be heard. I would have liked to read, but in a nearby garden an anti-aircraft gun went to work in such a deafening manner that I had to plug my ears with my index fingers and shut my eyes. An hour later the liberating siren began to howl and I could continue my journey. There was a crowd of about five hundred in front of the Legation's villa. The front gate was locked and the crowd had raised an ugly uproar; everyone was waving documents of one sort or another. From behind the iron bars of the fence the gatekeeper looked on with a bored expression. There was a policeman, equally apathetic, who took the trouble to explain to newcomers that there were too many people inside, and that clients were admitted in groups of ten. I stood a way back in the street to see what would happen. This proved to be a great stroke of luck. Five minutes later a boy of about fifteen stepped out of the villa and, on seeing me, motioned to me to come in on the right side. This young man led the writer through the neighbouring villa and into the Legation, skilfully managing to shut the gate just before the others who ran after us got there. He happened to be the son of the gentleman who was issuing the protective passes. This Mr Forgács received me by reciting a stanza from one of my oldest poems (one that I am a bit embarrassed of by now). As a matter of course, and with the greatest considerateness, he issued my Swedish pass, and the same for my brother and sisters. As it turned out we did not even need a Swedish sponsor, since we were placed on the artists' list. We were even exempted from the usual fees. Mr Forgács told me that he had been hauled in by the Gestapo several times; they resented this relief action on behalf of the Jews. Each time the Ambassador had to secure his release from incarceration. But not even the Ambassador was safe here. He also told me that most people applying for Swedish protection offered bribes of 5, 10 or 20,000 pengős. One lady, upon introducing herself, tried to palm off a 10,000-pengő banknote on him.

After that my sister delivered the necessary photos at the Legation. On the way back, this sister of mine, who is a teacher, met an old classmate of hers. Her colleague said how sorry she was that my sister had to wear a yellow star – she never realized she had the misfortune of being Jewish.

'I have the small consolation,' my sister told her, 'of knowing that some of my students, who by the way were unaware that I am Jewish, still think of me with affection, and still write touching letters from time to time.'

She must have said this in a voice louder than necessary, because when they reached Gellért Square up jumped an elderly woman dressed in mourning who had been following them, and, shouting for a policeman, she pointed out my sister.

'This Jewess has been flagrantly maligning our nation. She was telling her friend that this is a filthy dirty country and hopes the Hungarian army is beaten. Arrest her!'

A small crowd gathered; the colleague vanished the minute the policeman arrived. My sister, gathering her wits after the initial shock, stepped up to a colonel who happened to be coming that way, and who seemed like a decent sort.

'Sir, this woman is trying to trump up some awful charge against me. I swear to God I said nothing of the sort. You are a gentleman; please do not allow an innocent person to be dragged off to the police station.'

The decent colonel screamed at my sister:

'Filthy rotten Jews, into the Danube with you!'

The woman in black kept up her squawking and the policeman led my sister away. After being incarcerated from noon till evening, she was led in front of a police clerk, who said this to her once they were alone:

'Madam, I am convinced that the woman who denounced you was not speaking the truth. There are many cases like this every day. Unfortunately we have to convict every person (Jews, that is) who has been denounced, because the Germans check our records. I am going to mete out the lightest sentence, which is police surveillance.'

After that my sister had to report at the police station every Monday to verify that she was still living at her current address.

Along with all the ominous news we received some that was almost heartening, chiefly from Mr B. (import-export). One day he came back to report that all converted Jews would be exempted from wearing the yellow star, thanks to the Catholic Primate. Mr B. had it straight from a prominent politician, with whom he had served in the army, and whom he happened to meet on the street. 'I predict,' said the man, 'that by the first of the month all converted Jews will be exempted from the star. Hungary has too much to atone for already. The gentlemen in power are in a great panic ready to do anything to create some sympathy among the Allied powers.' A few days after that, Mr B. sprung his next great sensation: Romania was about to sue for peace. The negotiations were still in progress, that's why it hadn't been in the news from Moscow, London or New York. Mr B. had just received the news from Switzerland but couldn't reveal his source. The gentlemen listening to him smiled at each other; by now they all knew that Mr B. manufactured his rosy news. In fact, in our building, when people heard news that wasn't quite trustworthy, they would label it a 'B.-type broadcast'.

As for me, I liked a man who dreamed on behalf of his fellows, I liked fibs that were pleasant to hear. I had also learned lately that if someone dared to serve up a turn of events that was not quite a fact, then that event was usually about to happen. The future speaks through the mouth of the imagination.

I think it must have been towards the end of August

when that dear vagabond, the writer Tersánszky, visited me after ferreting out my address. He said he came bearing bad news. Sooner or later the Germans would take away the Jews of Budapest. But perhaps those who were converted would be saved by the Primate. (There was even a rumour of a threatened Papal interdict on Hungary.) In any case, I should convert. He had already arranged it with a friend of his, a priest, who would do it without the required wait. Well, I did not make use of this kind offer, and stayed a Jew among the other Jews. When I mentioned Tersánszky's thoughtfulness to Messrs T. and F., the latter admitted that he, the pious Jew, had already undergone conversion, together with his mother and sister, although these two had not the least idea that they were now Christians. He had an ambitious Gentile lawyer arrange the formalities for them, for a goodly sum of money. He did not study the catechism, nor did he ever see a priest; the lawyer delivered the baptismal certificates at his door. One never knew if this conversion might not come in handy; as far as the ethical side went, Mr F. opined:

'I am trying to protect our lives against a band of murderers. This is not an issue of fair play.'

He said they already had Swedish and Swiss papers, for what they were worth. According to him, the Governor's letter of exemption could not be taken seriously: why should the Germans respect it?

And I had made arrangements at the Swedish Legation, when I went there, to return the Swedish pass after I received the Governor's exemption . . . For some reason I believed the two kinds of protection nullified each other.

In September, when they were still investigating whether I had ever been a communist, I became so disgusted with the whole affair that I sent my sister to retrieve my petition. No Governor's exemption for me, thank you.

By then thousands and thousands of anxious Jews in Budapest had not only Swedish and Swiss passes but Portuguese as well! It was a question of money. The Swiss pass, they said, was the cheapest, could be had for 5,000. The Portuguese, for now, were asking at least 10,000. (A little later Spanish passes came into vogue, and became the popular favourite, like some flashy flamenco dancer.) Poor Jews, poor rich Jews, who swore by the efficacy of Spanish protection against German abuse. At the very worst, you might have to emigrate to Spain.

In September the gendarmes were gone again and then once more they reappeared. Boring, isn't it? Meanwhile the front lines seemed to have frozen, the Brits and Russians were stalled. The Russians had been at Königsberg for two months and the British seemed unwilling to move past Ancona. Mr T. thought maybe they were considering going up to Venice; or else they could be waiting for more ships. We who were living under constant threat found this tarrying most disheartening to behold. The British and Russian armies seemed to be acting like a fly that scurried about on a newspaper only to suddenly stop and stand still as if it were trying to read.

I wish to express my gratitude to the author of a book I was reading at this time; his name, till then not familiar to me, is Clarence Day. His book, *Life with Father*, reminisces about life in the good old days. His tales about the way his parents dealt with the telephone in their home made me laugh out loud more than once. Back when contact via the telephone line was still a novelty, the clumsy contraption was delegated to the parlour or the kitchen. (To make a call you had to crank up the set.) The telephone was handled by the maid or the cook; genteel folk did not personally speak through the phone. When the father wanted to arrange an afternoon meeting with someone, the maid had to come and go four or five times conveying questions and answers. Or else when the mother discussed with a friend what to wear for the theatre, the cook had to make forty or fifty trips from kitchen to living room and back. There was an old cook who would not touch the devilish contraption for anything.

What a blessing those few days were, while the book lasted. I hope Clarence Day Esq. is still alive; he must be an old man, but let him live to be older, may he rest without sleeping pills, may his stomach and heart be sound and may he smoke his cigars undisturbed.

We were terribly saddened by the fate of a charming 12-year-old boy in our building, whose mother sent him out one morning to pick fruit in the garden of their villa on the outskirts of town. The child was caught by the gendarmes who took him away. For days on end the desperate mother went running all over the place, but no trace of the child. (The father had been taken to the Russian front.) The poor woman cried night and day, blaming herself, suicidal. I couldn't bear to confront her; I didn't know what to say to her.

It was not for the first time that I heard about Jews being taken to the gas chambers in Germany. But I did not believe it. And I still cannot believe it. Deep down I cannot believe it, I just cannot.

October

The Jewish High Holy Days arrived at the end of September and the beginning of October. For the two days of the New Year and the sacred day of the Yom Kippur fast Mr F.

invited all of his friends from our building and the apartment house next door. In order to spare his ailing mother the fatigue of going to the temple, he rented a Torah scroll and retained a young cantor for the holy days. (The cantor had been granted High Holy Days leave from the factory where he was doing forced labour.) Out of politeness I attended the private services on the sacred days for an hour; I had no patience for staying longer. All morning and afternoon the believers were at their Hebrew prayer-books. There were lady guests as well, properly separated from the menfolk in their own room, the door kept open, naturally. For these days, the Jewish population was given the freedom of the streets from eight in the morning to seven at night.

Heathen though I was, my heart was stirred by the hum emanating from the bent, covered heads, and the loud chanting of the Torah that I had heard so often in my childhood. The ladies next door whispered their prayers; the good Lord alone knows how much of it they understood. They were diligently dabbing at their eyes and faces with tiny handkerchiefs. One of the guests there was a fellow-tenant, Mr G., who had become a Roman Catholic convert many years ago. Of course it was not thought proper to invite the converted Jews but he had asked permission to participate in the services. He brought his own prayer-book and even wore the full-length, white linen robe for the occasion. (Pious Jews are buried in these.) He devoutly whispered and murmured the Hebrew texts all day long. There was no harm in this; God the Roman Catholic Father is not jealous of Jehova.

Around that time came the news that the Governor had dissolved the government and was appointing a six-member council of generals.* Now who would these be? Everyone had

* Horthy fired the Sztójay government on 28 August, when the more moderate General Lakatos was appointed Prime Minister.

heard different names. (I no longer recall a single one of them.) Of course the first question asked by the Jews was the one asked by Klein when Grosz tells him the giraffe has escaped from the zoo: 'But how will this affect us?'

Naturally enough all these thoughtful gentlemen in our building, in addition to their own misfortunes were also deeply concerned about their country; the terrible ravages sustained each passing day which were bound to have lasting effects for future years. The Russians were knocking at the gates of Debrecen, the Germans were still lording it over us, and there was the awful devastation caused by Allied bombing night and day. Who could keep count of the factories destroyed, the fine mansions and villas in ruins? Gone were the Museum of Fine Arts, the Museum of the Capital, the Millennial Monument. What would be left of our beautiful Budapest?

A lighter note was provided in those days of dire peril by the increasing numbers of Jewish boys, sans forced labour armbands, sneaking home for the evening meal, and all those husbands on unauthorized leave from the war plants for the night. And the most brazen ones were invariably the most Jewish-looking – they were somehow always convinced that they 'did not look at all like Jews'. Also the yellow-starred women going to market during the curfew without wearing their stars: how could they get away with it? In our building many were exempted from wearing the yellow star, thanks to Swedish or Swiss passes. Policemen were often lenient when they caught someone wearing a star hurrying home after the five o'clock curfew. Even when vengeful Gentiles demanded the arrest of a Jew, the policeman sometimes merely pretended to write out a ticket and then waved him on to go home in peace.

The Fifteenth of October

Once again we saw the justification of the wishful 'B.-type broadcast' and of my own theories. Five or six days previously, Mr B. had reported that Governor Horthy was suing for peace, and had been negotiating with the British for days. Of course he was unable to name his source. Even hard-core pessimists began to believe this 'B.-type broadcast', since calling for a cease-fire was such a plausible move. There was much gladness and rejoicing. But a few of us realized, with a shudder, that the Germans were still here, and would seize control of the country.

Well, on 15 October, after lunch, one of my sisters rushed into the room and threw her arms around my neck.

'Peace! Peace at last! We asked for a cease-fire!' she exclaimed with tears in her eyes.

I looked out of the window but the park and the bridge appeared to be pretty much the same as before.

A few minutes later there was a knock at the door. It was Mr B.

'Maestro, forgive me for disturbing you, but you are invited at nine this evening to partake of five bottles of champagne I've been saving for this day. What do you say? You see, you can rely on the "B.-type broadcast".'

My sisters came back from the neighbours with news that the whole house was busy unstitching the yellow stars (those that were left). Dr H. even ran downstairs to the janitor, demanding the yellow star be removed from the front entrance. When the janitor balked, Dr H. threatened to slap his face, whereupon the ladder was duly brought, and the house was no longer marked by a yellow star. The tenants were thronging the stairs and corridors; all of Israel was rejoicing.

I did not feel like talking to anyone, lest my ugly

anxieties be revealed.

Around three in the afternoon the apartment commander came in to convey a message from Mr K., the building commander: would all of the gentlemen be good enough to pay him a visit on the sixth floor.

His living room was crammed full of people. He had called the meeting because there was a chance that armed extremist elements might attempt to break into the building. The entrance had already been locked (after it was flung wide open in the first flush of wild jubilation) and the yellow star replaced above it. Taking it down had been premature. Now we had to prepare the defence of the building. We had four firearms: one shotgun and three pistols. We were invited to use whatever we could find: hatchets, iron rods, kitchen knives, cleavers, pestles, iron-tipped sticks, whatever was on hand. When the watch blew the whistle, we were to take up our positions on the stairway landings of each floor. The rest was in the hands of the good Lord.

The gentlemen promptly armed themselves. To be sure, already in the course of the meeting we could hear artillery fire from here and there, gunshots, staccato machine-gun fire pounding like a clattering typewriter. What could this be? Who was shooting and why?

Around four Mr T. came upstairs with disheartening news: incomprehensibly the radio had been playing only military marches for the past quarter of an hour. Something was amiss.

But, alas, it was all over by then. The Germans had placed the government of the 1,000-year-old Hungarian kingdom in the hands of Szálasi.*

* Governor Horthy's declaration on Hungarian Radio of the cessation of hostilities was quickly followed by an Arrow Cross putsch, supported by German troops. Horthy was removed to Germany, a virtual prisoner, and Szálasi took over as 'National Leader' during the last months of the war.

The Arrow Cross government started out by declaring total curfew restricting Jews to their buildings, and invalidating all letters of exemption and protective passes issued by the Governor or by foreign states. Every Jew had to sew back the yellow star.

Fortunately my sisters had saved our stars when we received our Swedish passes. There was much hurried improvising in those apartments where the stars had been thrown out.

All summer long I had watched how those yellow stars were cared for: washed and ironed, cleaned with spot remover if stained, then reversed and sewn back on. And some ladies or gentlemen used lemon yellow, some yellow ochre, depending on what went well with what coat. And certain finicky dames and dandies wore yellow silk, much more elegant than the linen or cotton ones.

So we were locked in for five days; we could read in the papers about the myriad new government appointments and decrees. No one dared to smuggle food into our building during those five days. And then on the sixth day . . .

'Your mother's . . .'

There we were, marching out, on 20 October.

It was a bit strange that they led us away from the centre of the city, towards the Újpest outskirts. Up at the head of the column marched the policeman and the corporal; the four others flanked us, two on each side. We were proceeding in good marching order, at least we were trying to, but our slave-drivers soon began to scream out from either side:

'Stay in step, excellencies!'

'Step lively back there, your mother's . . .' (This voice belonged to the youngest guard.)

'Chin up, old Moses!'

'Keep in step, you're lagging behind!'

Their eyes did not leave us for a second.

Passers-by on the sidewalk and in the street turned to stare at us; in streetcars some women even stood up from their seats to get a better view of us down to our shoes. One carter with a cart-load of sacks loudly laughed at us, and one or two among the passers-by watched our procession with a smile of satisfaction. But most people, after giving us a cursory look, went on their way; they had worries other than the Jews.

'What's going on, straggling back there!'

'What a herd of pigs!'

'Straighten that line!'

'Let's go, Abe, stop dragging your feet!'

'Close your ranks, you goddam dirty Jew, or I'll show you!'

For the duration of the march these jeers rang out from all sides every minute or two. We marched past the new Leopoldstadt to Lehel Square, from there to Arena Road, then Thököly Road, where we had to wait while a column of gigantic German armoured cars daubed with yellow and green camouflage clattered and rattled by. Watching them were a few pedestrians, and one policeman. He turned to one of the older gentlemen wearing a yellow star:

'Sir, how old are you?'

The old man dared not answer, merely smiled in embarrassment.

The policeman stepped up to one of the soldiers escorting us.

'Look, this man over here is surely over sixty years old. I saw the orders this morning, it said you are supposed to take men under sixty. There are several here older than that, how come you are taking them too?'

Well, that brat of a young soldier merely waved off the police officer, who must have been around forty-two or forty-four, and had a handsome Hungarian face.

'That's none of your business, mind the traffic.'

The policeman clenched his jaw and stared hard at the soldier for about twenty seconds, then turned and walked away without a word.

Several of the gentlemen over sixty had already exchanged hopeful glances.

When the last armoured car had gone by, we marched on, to Kerepesi Road, where we came to the entrance to the 'Kisok' soccer field. But we did not stop there – they herded us in.

The Sports Ground

This had once been a sports compound for high school students, a giant rectangular field, big enough for who knows how many soccer fields. It had been overgrown by weeds in the years since students' cheers were last heard here.

What a vast gathering! Everyone standing in columns facing the grandstand. Our escort led us to the end of one column and left us there without a word of goodbye. As it turned out, this column and the two to the right were all made up of men from the Fifth District. That's how they arrayed us, according to districts. About two-thirds of the field was filled with a mass of humanity. In front of the grandstand, with their backs to our columns, was another throng. Ahead of us, behind us, and on all sides we were surrounded by police and soldiers and armed men wearing Arrow Cross armbands; they strolled about to keep order, i.e. made sure that no one escaped. An additional half a dozen braves with fixed bayonets stood guard by the gates.

How many of us were on that field? I am not good at that kind of estimate; we could have been 20,000 – or 50,000 strong.* One gentleman near me said 25,000, another, 35,000, a third guessed 40,000, while a fourth didn't think there were more than 12,000 of us. (A stingy soul, no doubt.) There were fresh detachments pouring through the two gates, coming from the direction of town, and they were all added on to one column or another.

What were we doing here? We just stood around, waiting. We were allowed to talk to each other and to smoke. I noticed a dear friend, a painter, two columns over on the left, and stepped out into the free space between two columns to yell 'Fritzi! Fritzi!' at the top of my voice. He didn't hear. When I tried to work my way over to where he was standing, a civilian guard stopped me.

'No visiting allowed.'

'And what if I offer you a fine Darling cigarette?'

'Not even then.'

But he courteously accepted the offered cigarette.

On all sides people were greeting and waving at acquaintances glimpsed. The momentary smiles of pleasurable recognition were quickly displaced by helpless, confused glances. The main topic of conversation: what could be going on by that grandstand? The consensus was that the conscription was taking place there – at which doctors would send home all people with infirmities.

---

* 'Altogether some fifty thousand recruits were marched off to a racecourse and a sports-ground.' John Bierman, *Righteous Gentile: The Story of Raoul Wallenberg* (London: Bantam Books, 1983), p. 79.

'I swear they'll have to let me go, I've got severe diabetes.'

'Me too, I should be able to get off with my asthmatic heart condition.'

'Strange, I don't see anyone moving in that crowd in front of the grandstand. Not a soul is coming back.'

'Perhaps the doctors are not here yet.'

'If you ask me, there is no conscription here, can't you see they are bringing up a new bunch every few minutes? They are simply distributing the units there, forwarding them on, or something.'

Well, we would find out soon enough. Many of the gentlemen were already going through their wallets for medical certificates and prescriptions.

It occurred to me that I had forgotten to wind my watch. I usually do that at nine in the morning. Next, I discovered that I had left my watch at home. Darn it, I had never been without a watch since my student years (except for those occasions in my youth when I had had to place it in hock).

What time was it? Half past nine. We arrived here at nine. How long did we have to wait and wait here, and who knows what for?

Troop after troop marched towards the grandstand, and others came from the opposite direction; new groups kept pouring through the gates and forming into columns; all this movement resembled tattered clouds driven before a storm. What went on near that grandstand remained a mystery, in spite of all our speculations. We could see that more and more people were sitting down on the grass, everyone was tired. Among us, too, some were already sitting on their rucksacks. Looking around I noticed faces familiar from restaurants, opera audiences or the sidewalks – there were many I knew by sight. And every minute I saw some personal acquaintance far off – editors, actors, businessmen, doctors, lawyers, film-makers, waiters, storekeepers, men from all walks of life. There was not much talking, most were just standing and gaping around like myself, or were absorbed in staring at the ground. I wished this whole multitude could have got down on all fours and turned into sheep, to crop the grass from morning to night, without ever having to think.

The boredom was lethal, and I had nothing to read. I felt like lying down for a nap. I put down my knapsack, placed the blanket on top: so long, world! But sleep would not come, what with the shouts on all sides, the wail of a locomotive, the grinding of a streetcar's wheels and the occasional infernal detonation of a truck tyre blowing out. So I ended up watching the ocean of cloudless sky. Suddenly there were shouts and a commotion all around: supposedly they were rounding up everyone aged sixty and over. Well, at last! I had turned sixty only weeks before. Even to think about it was horrible. Or rather the horror lay mostly in thinking about it, for in reality one feels little difference between yesterday and today. Actually I felt no different than when I was thirty.

Almost all of the gentlemen from Pozsonyi Road were grabbing their bags: most of them were past sixty. Anyone younger than that among us had to be a disabled veteran, or else officially recognized for counter-revolutionary merit, or engaged in the defence industry. Of course they too firmly believed that they would not be taken anywhere and had the papers to prove it.

Word had it that all of us aged sixty and over had to march up to the grandstand. Off to the side I caught a glimpse of a dear friend of mine, the graphic artist Laci Reiter, who was only about forty-eight. He had been a great one for sojourning in Paris, where he would spend six months at a time, sitting by the Dôme all night long, smoking a cigar. He would listen to the half-crazy artists of the Dôme; even when sitting with a female companion he just smoked his cigar, without a word. (After this encounter at the sports ground I did not see him again until the following July, when he came home at last.) By the time I took my leave of Laci, my companions from Pozsonyi Road had already been moved on. I had to forge my way through the crowd massed in front of the grandstand, and was shoved back repeatedly. I fought my way through that multitude, only to find another thick mass of humanity directly in front of the grandstand. Once there, one of the more patient gentlemen informed me that the call for 60-year-olds had been a false alarm. I see. Now I had to struggle back through that thicket of humans, back to where I had started from. I had no idea where my group was and ran up and down from one column to another, in search of my companions from Pozsonyi Road.

'No, we are from the Second District!'

'What do you want here, this is the Eighth District!'

And every minute some civilian guard or soldier yelled at me to stop loitering and get back in place. I must have wandered around in a daze for about half an hour when in between two columns I noticed a white handkerchief waving. It belonged to Herr Direktor V., who must have had some pair of eyeglasses to pick me out from so far away. There they were, all in place, my companions. So I dragged myself over there; on the way, one youth wearing an armband raised his whip against me. I was so tired that I immediately lay down by my knapsack.

About half the folks were sitting down on the grass, many were trying to sleep, others nibbled provisions. So we sat and stood waiting. It was nearly half past eleven. What was going to happen here? The uncertainty alone was enough to drive you crazy. Again I discovered familiar faces in the distance: one a conductor, the other a banker dressed up to the nines, leaning on his walking stick, staring at his special hiking boots. He cut a most exclusive figure; how was he going to get along in this mixed crowd, when they took him away? Each moment there was someone else to pity.

By noon we finally found out that there was to be no medical examination whatsoever (this news passed from troop to troop). All of us here would be taken away, and they were only distributing the groups in front of the grandstand, assigning where they were to be sent. Poor Mr T. by my side was awfully thirsty; he claimed he would pay a tenner for a glass of water. It was beginning to get quite warm, almost like summer. Left and right everyone was yawning, all this waiting was unspeakably boring. I was amazed that I had not started howling in desperation and charging blindly at the world at large, like a wild bull on the plains of Hortobágy. They were making us stand around with the sole purpose of driving us crazy. That mysterious committee or whatever in front of the grandstand was straight out of Reinhardt; our fates lay in the hands of those invisible ones who tormented us, and passed judgment. Everyone was facing in that direction, confronting our Doom.

Around 1 p.m. men wearing Arrow Cross armbands approached us from the direction of the grandstand. They marched down among the columns, shouting:

'All those over sixty, line up by the fence!'

Well, at last the 60-year-olds from Pozsonyi Road breathed a sigh of relief. And a hopeful buzz arose on all sides.

We fell into formation, because all the other groups had started to move in formation. Behind us came other troops from the Fifth District. On the short march over to the edge of the field the conversation took on a more relaxed tone.

'Lucky for them, because I was just beginning to lose

my patience!'

'We'll be home just in time for dinner. Am I going to stuff myself!'

'Didn't I tell you nothing was going to happen?' (That was Mr B.)

'That policeman was right, after all, about the 60-year age limit. We were taken from the building out of sheer malice. We had to come all the way here to the soccer field to find out.'

There by the fence was an endlessly long column, four men abreast. We had about a dozen guards at either end. Facing the gate, we stood and stood, waiting. We had waited a quarter of an hour already when a civilian sporting a Hitler moustache appeared, clad in yellow leather, complete with boots, armband and bludgeon. Making a megaphone out of his hands, he bawled at us:

'All those over sixty, hold up your papers!'

Everyone reached for their wallets.

Poor Mr T. and Herr Direktor V. got left behind on the field; they were both under sixty.

Mr K., a postal official aged 72, dropped like a frail, tired autumn leaf. He could not stay on his feet any longer.

Up stepped the leather-coat and called out in a kind of pidgin German.

'*Nü tate zisse, vass iz? Shvach auf di brust!*' ('What's up, pops? Chin up!')

The old man did not answer, his small blue eyes sadly fixed on the giant revolver holstered on his questioner's side. The latter addressed him again, with seemingly endless cheer.

'*Un vass macht di mame zisse? Ha? Hörn zö möch nish?*' ('And what's mama doing? Eh? Can't you hear me?')

He chuckled at the downed man, and made as if to hit him with the bludgeon.

'Please, I don't understand what you are saying,' the

fallen man said, with such agitation and trembling of head and hands that we were seriously worried on his behalf.

'Of course you understand me, gramps, I'm trying to talk your language.'

'But I understand only Hungarian.'

'*Ts, ts, ts! Gott über di velt!*' ('Tsk, tsk, tsk! God in his heaven!') Now the leather-coated man started to mimic the old man's trembling head and hands. With a robust guffaw, he kept looking back at the rest of the company, waiting for us to share his merriment. Then he glanced at the downed man again with a kind of cheerful scorn, and again waved his shiny, brand-new bludgeon over him, as if undecided. His expression grew severe, and he roared out:

'Get up now!'

Then he turned around, and strolled on. We could hear his voice shrilling in the back.

'Hey, what do you think you're doing there?'

An older man was taking a leak against the fence.

'Turn around! Face the brothers of your race! That's right!'

And he howled once more:

'Don't you dare hide it! Hold it up now!'

One gentleman remarked in an undertone:

'I'd love to hang this one myself.'

Again he was walking our way, constantly flapping and smacking his bludgeon.

'Stand up straight and tall! Stop leaning on your walking stick like you do at home on your Persian carpets!'

He moved on, then thought of something else.

'Put those knapsacks back on! At the double!'

Many people had removed these and placed them on the ground.

Oh, it would be so sweet to be heading back home.

Here came an armed corporal. At last we were leaving. But no.

'If you're seventy or over, step out here on this side!'

He marched on, yelling the same thing over and over along the length of our column.

Two elderly gentlemen stepped forth out of our group.

What was the meaning of this?

The consensus was that they would probably take the older ones back on a streetcar; the march would be too much for them.

We were still standing and waiting. There was a whispered debate about whether smoking was allowed. Someone saw smoke in the next troop, and immediately the cigarette cases were opened and offered to neighbours: have a smoke!

Since we had been directed here, the whole field had begun to convulse with movement: every minute a new troop would set out, under guard, through one of the two gates. In each departing troop heads turned our way and hands were raised in farewell. I saw the tall Nándor Szücs, editor of *The News*, black patch over one of his eyes, looking back, not finding the person to whom he wanted to say goodbye.

Now a sergeant was approaching. He would surely set us on our way homeward. It was late enough: almost two already.

With bayonet fixed the sergeant halted near us and let out a shout for the benefit of the entire column.

'*Atten-shun!* Will you throw that cigarette down, you filthy pig, goddam your mother's bloody . . .! Straighten out! I want to see straight lines! Move in, you stinking swine!'

He waited until row after row moved up, and bellowed:

'Forward march!'

He hurried forward to the head of the column at the gate. The leather-clad civilian disappeared.

Oh yes, our good sergeant had seen to it that the 70-year-olds returned to their places in our column.

Now What?

So we marched out through the gate, and suddenly we noticed that the column was heading not in the direction of the Eastern Railway Station, but away from town, out towards Kerepesi Road.

This seemed an idiotically roundabout way of bringing home all these dead-tired people!

On both sides of the column marched soldiers with fixed bayonets.

We trudged on, and there was no about-face, no turn-off into some side street that would lead back to town. (For we were hoping that we had to make this detour because of the heavy traffic around the Station.) But we just kept marching forward.

We began to worry again. Could they be taking us somewhere else? The men were still clutching identity papers showing their birthdates. Someone a few rows back decided to risk addressing one of the soldiers marching by our side.

'Officer, would you kindly tell us where we are heading?'

The answer came after a moment's deliberation.

'You think I know?'

Back when we were still milling around on the sports field, one of our neighbours from Pozsonyi Road did tell us that word had it around the grandstands that we were being taken to forced labour on the outskirts of town, around Budakeszi and Ferihegy. But we had conveniently forgotten this.

In cautious undertones (lest we be yelled at) we began to voice guesses about what was happening to us. Were we, after all, being taken away? It had to be some sort of mistake. Or could they still turn us around in the direction of home? Some of us, including myself, were still capable of harbouring such wild hopes. I was not closely acquainted with the three gentlemen marching by my side; we had only briefly met back in our courtyard, during a bombing raid. I sorely missed Mr T. and Herr Direktor V., who had been sent off in another group. My brother was also taken somewhere else. So I just listened to the conversation of these three. They thought that no matter where we were taken, it would be found out that the 60-year-olds had been conscripted illegally. And even if they kept us there, sooner or later we would see a doctor, and those with medical problems would be sent home. And what 60-year-old didn't have some medical problem? (Especially if you were a Jew, added one gentleman in a low voice, to the similarly restrained merriment of the others.) Others were ready to concede that they would try to do the work, but what kind of work could such worn-out people be expected to do? Speculation was rife on all sides. Some thought we would be merely held as hostages, others opined we would be taken to barracks, for office work. A third guess was somewhat pessimistic: they could take us to a farm, to husk corn, shell beans and peas, help out with farm machinery, or pluck feathers. We could put up with all of that for a time; after all, how long could this go on? (Someone remarked he had great childhood practice at feather-plucking.) And the good gentlemen lapsed into all kinds of rural daydreams: it wouldn't be such a bad idea to live for a while among peasants, see farm animals, horses, sheep, cattle. Someone remarked that there is nothing like roasting bacon by a camp-fire, dripping the fat on a slice of toasted bread; add a gulp of cool white wine and it beat the finest dinner, gentlemen! As to the question of where we would be quartered, the same man answered: 'in farmhouses'.

We marched on in a somewhat resigned mood, the only sour note being the periodic shouts of our military escort on the left or right, reminding us to straighten out and step lively. It was a warm day. Some gentlemen were wiping their foreheads, many had taken off their hats. We marched on the side of the road. Occasionally we had to crowd over, when large trucks or armoured vehicles rumbled by. The drivers, Hungarian or German soldiers, looked down at us with indifference. Those passing us on carts or on foot all gave us the once-over; occasionally a child or an old woman lugging a sack or a basket stopped to stare better. We did not hear any comments. Only two young housewives giggled on seeing us. I couldn't say that their laughter was prompted by scorn or hatred – it was merely childish and unthinking. They laughed because we were being driven like helpless cattle.

We marched for an hour, two hours. We lost track of the time. The streets had been left behind us long ago. We had been so exhausted when we set out, but amazingly we still kept marching. We got the hang of it. But various minor problems began to arise. The man on my right kept saying he was dying for a drink of water. This gentleman used to be a wholesaler. (By now I had had a chance to exchange a word or two with my neighbours.) The one on the left had a nail bothering his foot; it was beginning to be torture. The man ahead of me kept reaching back under his weighty knapsack: the straps were cutting into his shoulder. He wore a thin overcoat. Left and right we passed scattered small railway shacks, humble and homely villas, half-built houses that would not be completed for some time. Some of the buildings had suffered bomb damage. On fences and walls we saw swastikas daubed in green paint, and Szálasi's name in capital letters. On wooden fences we saw more SZÁLASI scrawls in chalk, some with the *S* inverted. Other graffiti were faded by the years. I felt the onset of recurring nicotine cravings; of course smoking was out of the question.

Hats and Caps

We marched and marched and marched. My companions figured out that we were going towards Rákospalota. That was the direction, but hardly our destination. I kept myself amused by surveying the various headpieces worn in front of me. Grey hats and beige hats; beige was the most numerous, this colour having been the fashion for the past few years. One or two elderly gentlemen wore hats with those very narrow brims, such as worn by young punks. But there were a few black hats visible – strange, in warm October weather. You could see plenty of caps as well: golfers' caps, touring caps for the sportier types. Oh, those fine wool travel caps, once in my foolish youth I bought one of those for a trip abroad. But I saw ahead of me many other types of caps, cheaper kinds worn by so-called 'little men' – retailers, artisans, workers, street vendors and poor peasants. Herr Direktor T. (who wore a cap whenever he went out on rubble clean-up details) kept me entertained once by giving an account of the cap industry: how small manufacturers bought up the remnants of inexpensive fabrics and linings, what a lively and competitive industry this was, and what a huge part of society Europe-wide and worldwide wore caps instead of hats. And that was not even counting all those students, scouts, soldiers, railroad employees, sailors, pilots, doormen and others who did not wear hats as a rule. If you were to hold a headcount you would find that more people on earth wore caps than hats.

I don't know what time it was when we arrived in Rákospalota. The main street was awfully long. I recalled speeding down that street in a car once or twice in the past, but it did not seem anywhere near as long then. Many stores, shoe shops, tailor's shops, laundries, bakeries were shut down; these businesses belonged to Jews. It seemed that about every third house had suffered some bomb damage. It is horrible that bombs make no distinctions: they destroy humble, tiny one-storey houses just the same. That infernal sneeze scatters walls, doors, windows, beds, tables, chairs; shatters plates, pitchers, basins, everything, all the belongings of struggling poor working folk. This was the same horrifying sight that had been depicted in issues of *Illustration* showing the outskirts of Paris after air raids.

We were boiling in the heat and our shoes were coated with a layer of dust; I also began to realize how hungry I was. I had forgotten that I had had nothing to eat since the crack of dawn. I will forgo mentioning all the reminders screamed at us from left and right about getting in step, stop bouncing, keep moving, accompanied by choice curses from our escort. Fortunately there were no ladies present. Here too the passersby on the sidewalk looked us over; they stopped, especially the children, to stare at the wanderers.

When would they let us rest?

Well, it finally occurred to them around five. Probably even our guards felt the need for a little siesta by then. They gave us half an hour. There was a shallow ditch by the roadside, it made us happy to sit down and dangle our feet in there.

Many sneaked off for a minute into a side street, among the ruins of bombed-out houses. As soon as people were seated, out came the provisions and the pocket knives. Bacon, canned food, chicken legs, cheeses, biscuits, fruit appeared on papers spread out in people's laps. But you could also see others eating only bread and an apple or onion. Soon the smokers lit up. Someone went into a store across the street, and came out with a stack of postcards which he handed out without accepting any money. So everyone started writing home, placing the cards on the sidewalk. We knew all too well that our half-hour would soon be over, like every other half-hour in our life; still, the order to get up came as a wretched shock. How difficult that was, to hoist oneself up again! Some of the older gentlemen fell back four or five times before they could stand up. There was a general rush to deposit the cards into a nearby mailbox. We all wrote that we were well, and on the way to do light labour.

That Large, Burly Man

We were off again. After a few steps, an older gentleman three rows ahead of me handed his postcard to a little girl about ten years old, who happened to be standing in the middle of the road. (He apparently hadn't had a chance to place it in the mailbox.)

'Please mail it for me, sweetheart.'

In that instant, a large, burly man of about fifty leaped over from the opposite sidewalk, knocked the postcard out of the old gentleman's hand, and landed a terrific slap on his face. This blow was delivered with an engineer's precision so that it hit squarely in the old gentleman's face; I could see the flash of a broad silver ring on the man's index finger. Never in my life had I seen or heard such a resounding slap. Three or four companions sprang to support the old man, who staggered, and would have fallen, were it not for his helpers, who linked arms with him on either side. And that large, burly man remained standing there, staring after the old gentleman with such a grim expression that you would have thought he was the one who suffered the blow in the face. I looked back at him to memorize his visage, in case we were to meet again in life.

We trudged on, saddened; no one spoke a word. That old man kept dabbing his eyes with his fist – he didn't dare to pull out a handkerchief. After a quarter of an hour's march, our escort started in again:

'You're dragging yourselves like lice. Straighten up!'

'Look at this crooked Jewish row!'

'You're lagging behind, grandpa! Want me to jump on your back?'

We were all dying of thirst. During our rest stop our brave escort had visited a tavern while we had not even been given water.

We dragged ourselves past Újpest.

I don't have to describe the remaining hours of the march for there were no amusing details to relate. It was a relief to see the occasional cyclist, a little foal tied to a cart, or hens pecking at a midden heap. The trees were fresh and green – it could have been May. Our military escort became more and more abusive: this long march was no joyride for them, either. Gradually evening descended on us. But there was no evening star. All around, the sky was overcast.

At the Racetrack

Around eight-thirty we arrived at the Káposztásmegyer racetrack. There we came to a halt. By then it had started to rain, a slow drizzle. I had personal reasons for a sigh: back in the First War, when I was a volunteer, we marched out here more than once on gorgeous spring mornings, learning how to ride and fall from a horse. Behind the grandstand there was a tavern where, after our exercises, we would eat hot dogs and rolls, and sip cold beer. Yes, the tavern was still there, but completely dark. Perhaps we could tap on the window for something to drink. But when one of the gentlemen approached a soldier about this, he was most rudely rebuked.

There stood our long column under the grandstand. No sign of any barracks where we could lie down. For this had to be where we were to stay for the night; how could they make all these exhausted people march on, in the rain? By now the drizzle had turned into full-fledged rain; long threads of water falling thick and fast, yet almost furtively. The cool wetness felt good on my hands and nose as I looked on, watching the gentle autumn rain. We stood there for fifteen or twenty minutes, without any sign of our guards. But we noticed the patch of light around the corner of the grandstands. Yes, they must have roused that tavern-keeper, and moved in there, *en masse*. They emerged about ten minutes later. The corporal stepped up in front of the column and began speechifying. The gist of it was, we were to sleep here. (But where? Perhaps there were some barracks hidden in the dark.) We had to arrange ourselves quietly, in good order, on the benches of the grandstand; we could relieve ourselves behind it. Anyone trying to escape would be shot. At five in the morning we were to stand here lined up. He did not want to hear any noise during the night, or else, etc. etc. Dismissed!

While he was talking, I kept tilting my head back to swallow the rain. All around me this was how everyone was drinking, like birds.

I can't say it was an unforgettable night because I would much rather forget it.

We started to climb the high steps of the grandstands, imagining we could lie down on the benches. But that was out of the question. There were too many of us. We had to sit up, closely packed together. If I placed my rucksack by my feet, there was no room for my feet in the narrow space. I had to keep it on my back or else in my lap. My back was hurting under that pack, and my shoulder ached where the straps dug in. As we stumbled up there one man after another fell; there was much shuffling, and hats, walking canes, packages were dropped. Flashlights were turned on. One of the braves, who was left behind to guard us while his comrades disappeared in the direction of the tavern, bawled out:

'Put out those damn lights, you traitorous Jews!'

And he immediately climbed up the steps.

'Hand over those flashlights! They'll be returned in the morning. If I find anyone hiding one, you are dead meat.'

He spent half an hour clambering over outstretched legs to collect every flashlight. (I had not brought one.) Meanwhile people were digging out their provisions from backpacks, suitcases, packages; paper was rustling on all sides. My neighbour on the left said he could not eat, he just wanted to sleep, sleep. And he leaned his head against me without as much as a by your leave. I managed to extricate my provisions and swallowed a bite of bread and plum jam. Smoking was not allowed; a lit match would have been taken as a signal for the Russians, British and Americans to drop their bombs on our heads. (I could never understand why the lighting of lamps and matches was not allowed at least until the first sound of the air-raid siren.) I leaned on my backpack, trying to sleep. In front of me, and all around, there was a continuous hissing. 'Please don't lean on me. Ouch, you're stepping on my foot. Please move over a little. Stop piling your things on me, I'm no coat rack.' There was much sighing and whispering, and someone was forever finding fault with his neighbour, amid arguments, squabbles and hisses on all sides calling for silence. I propped my head on my two fists, whereupon my neighbour's head dropped onto my backpack. He growled angrily and again placed his head on my shoulder. I felt so sorry for the man that I decided to put up with it. But now I could not lower my own head to rest. I tried to sleep in this manner. My neighbour on the right, what a genius! He was already asleep (although his arm was squeezing tight against mine). And how he snored! All around the grumbling was getting louder. I shut my eyes in the hope I would be able to fall asleep, for I was dead tired. But that was just it: I was too tired. This always happened when I had overworked myself or read too late into the night; I could not go to sleep for a long time. It was as if my nerves were inflamed. I kept trying to straighten out my waist, where I had a pain. The neighbour on the left again slid off my shoulder; half asleep, he growled at me and again leaned on me. Every minute brought more snores, snorts and hissing. What *naiveté*, to hiss at snorers! It appeared, at least judging by the sounds, that here and there a snorer was shaken awake, for the snoring would abruptly stop, to be followed by muted but all the more virulent sounds of squabbling. Someone fell with a resounding thud higher up; a walking cane bounced clattering down the steep steps; roused sleepers cried out or growled, heedless of the chorus of hisses. Suddenly our guard started to shout:

'What's going on here, I'm going to shoot if you don't shut up!' (This was followed by a string of most unseemly verbs and nouns, highly offensive to God and creatures made in his image.)

A relative quiet ensued, but the whispers and hisses kept up, and the snoring, too, from those happy ones who could sleep undisturbed. I don't know how long I sat there amusing myself by trying to harmonize all that random snoring. Suddenly I was jolted – I had fallen backwards and hit my head against a stone. It happened to be the rock-hard luggage of the man behind me. The poor man, whom I had woken, knocked his knee against my head and moaned miserably. So I must have fallen asleep. My neighbour on the left also woke and fell forward, having lost his support. I had to listen, all at once, to the complaints of the man behind, my neighbour on the left, and the unknown man in front, whose hat was crushed by the man on my left, whose head was on my shoulder again. So I sat up as straight as I could with open eyes; my back hurt, my waist hurt, and my neighbour's big head was a tormenting load on my shoulder. Earth and sky were one darkness; the rain was invisible and inaudible, but you could still feel it falling. I imagined the horse races at this track, the slim colts thudding by with those colourful monkeys squatting on their necks, and rosy clouds in the sky where no one was looking, all eyes popping at the sight of the horses. And everyone would start to roar and shout and laugh like at soccer games. Who knows how many elderly gents were sitting there at this moment in the same place they had occupied thirty or forty years ago, when they shouted the names of Taral and Janek in a trance. While I was thus submerged in the cavalcade a distant air-raid siren sounded – or it could have been a hallucination. It was amazing that no dogs were barking here. Were there no dogs at this place? I sat there, thinking; one is always thinking about something, always. And it isn't that a minute or two later you forget what had kept your mind occupied: sometimes you don't know what you are thinking even while you are having these faltering thoughts, even while you are thinking them. My head kept nodding forward each time my eyes closed for a moment or two. Some instinct kept me from falling over. Yet I still fell asleep for a brief spell; I could tell because during these snatches I had dreams. One of these mini-dreams stayed with me. I was strolling on a lawn in the company of a man with a long, white beard. Suddenly we stopped in front of a row of squatting men, their hands buried in the soil like so many spades. The white-haired man pointed at them: 'These, you see, are the murderers, *their hands are ripening.*' Then I woke up. The whole place seemed to be wrapped in fog, and those silent men in my dream had worn clothes the colour of fog. Of course this instructive little dream had something to do with the times, with the war going on.

My seat was wicked hard and there was nothing I could place under me. It felt like my nerves were on fire. In my boredom I had recourse to an old pastime: recalling poems. This is what I always do when I am caught on a bus without reading matter, or am the captive audience of a tiresome man or woman's endless tales. I look into their eyes with devotion so they think I am hanging on each word; at random intervals I laugh, or shake my head, or sigh. My favourite poets are Csokonai* and de Musset. And so I 'thought' my way through the poem called 'For Lilla, Once Again' – thank God it still went without a hitch. Then came de Musset's '*L'andalouse*'; how I would have loved to chant this fiery, mad poem out loud! I dared not sleep for fear of falling back or forwards. But my eyes kept shutting for a snippet of sleep every once in a while. I had a pain in the back of my neck, a dull, medullar headache I only get when I am totally exhausted. And I had no medicine

* Csokonai Vitéz, Mihály (1773 – 1805), lyric poet.

with me. My nerves were aflame. Those unfortunate older men whose bladders could not make it through the night were starting, one after another, to stumble their way down the steps, down to the field in the rain, stepping on sleepers' feet and triggering excruciating reproaches. The first one to reach the field was stopped at rifle point by our guard. Mercifully he did not fire, merely swore out loud, and allowed the ones following to pass in silence. Many beside me were unable to sleep; on all sides I kept hearing much sighing, coughing, clearing of throats and fidgeting. My God, how superfluous that others should suffer – wasn't my suffering enough? Even staying awake and watchful I kept falling backwards, I was becoming so weak. Yet I had to chuckle, in spite of my tormented back, waist, head, nerves. It seemed I had been sitting in the dark on this grandstand for months, years! I had no recall of ever doing anything else in life.

At 5 a.m. the guard roused up the audience in the grandstand. It was no longer pitch-black, but a dark dawn, the dawn of an overcast day.

Adding up all those snatches, I must have had half an hour's sleep.

Morning

The rain had stopped some twenty minutes ago. Lo and behold: something we could be thankful for. We dragged ourselves away from the grandstand; it took a quarter of an hour before everyone was on the field. Our guard then graciously granted permission for us to relieve ourselves. Some had already set off at a trot towards the fences, they just had to go. But the soldier yelled at them: 'Halt, about face! Whoever tries to escape will be shot! Line up on the grass!'

Behind the grandstand we discovered a well. Everyone grabbed their tin cups, untying them from the rucksacks where they were hung in military fashion. Tin cups and mugs and towels, soap, comb and brush, toothbrush and toothpaste. Some gentlemen were 'practical' enough to bring paper cups – they were clearly weekend hiking types. I, like many others, had no tin cup, but found a good sturdy mug my sister had stuffed between the shirts in my backpack. So I stood in line with that, to await my turn. But one of my fellow travellers on his way back was kind enough to fill my cup with water so I could start rinsing my mouth and having a wash.

When we were done with our ablutions, our guard pronounced permission for breakfast. Line-up at six! He was still the only representative of the armed forces on the field. The racetrack had been overrun by weeds – who knows when the last meet was held at Káposztásmegyer. People scattered; some sat in the grandstands, others plopped down on the grass on top of blankets or coats. Small cans were opened; papers or napkins spread; fried chicken was unwrapped, and bacon, salami, ham, butter, cheeses, including Liptauer; but many of the poorer sort ate only bread and plums, or bread and onion, or bread alone. I noticed that some of the gentlemen had brought thermos flasks; I must have seen two or three dozen. But how many shabby, worn overcoats, winter coats and dirty raincoats, and what decayed shoes, holes in the soles! There are only two nations in the world, two races, two religions: the rich and the poor. Soon enough, we were done with breakfast; everyone wanted to light one up before falling into formation. At 6 a.m. we

all crowded in front of the grandstand. A few of the gentlemen from the building on Pozsonyi Road turned up; we
talked and stayed together. Again the waiting began. We
waited and waited. I still had a headache, and pains in my
back, waist, thighs: good morning, muscle cramps. Herr
Direktor Nádas (one of those who stood next in line) had
given me a powder against the headache, but so far it had
had no effect.

At last, after another half-hour, the military showed
up: another set of fellows, not the same as the day before.
About ten soldiers, half of them wearing Arrow Cross armbands, the rest regular Army. Our night-time guard had evaporated as well. Right away one of the corporals shouted the
order:

'Fall in, and make it snappy!'

We shuffled and squirmed into a column four abreast,
our marching order of the day before. The corporal, who had
walked away in the meantime, now turned on us:

'By threes, goddammit, didn't you hear?'

In five minutes we had accomplished the rearrange-
ment. Then another corporal showed up, one who wore an
armband, and he screamed at us in a high-pitched, effeminate
voice:

'What's going on here? Line up by fours!'

The other soldiers were standing around, smoking in
front of the grandstand, looking us over, chuckling. And by
the way: they had forgotten to return the confiscated flashlights.

When we had formed our column, the corporal again
thought of something:

'Divide into platoons of one hundred! Three steps'
interval between platoons!'

So we counted ourselves off all the way down the line

and accomplished this division into platoons in another fifteen minutes.

By then the sun was shining, thank God.

But Where To?

It was past seven when they ordered us to march from the racetrack. The sound of bells floated from somewhere, a sweet and gentle tolling. The bells were still echoing in our ears when from our left and right soldiers started to shout.

'Keep in line! Step lively, gentlemen!' (This latter must have been a streetcar conductor in civilian life.)

Another echoed from the back:

'Close ranks! Stop lagging!'

I must warn the reader that I am going to bore you with these exhortations from the military, just as they bored us every few minutes.

The guessing game was going on in low voices: where could they be taking us? This was the Gödöllő highway, so we were probably going to Gödöllő,* according to Mr Aczél, commercial councillor, proprietor of the 'Indestructible' firm (whose trademark, ever since my childhood, had demonstrated the toughness of their blue overalls, tugged by three straining men on each side). How many kilometres to Gödöllő? About thirty. The councillor was my neighbour on the left; on my right marched Mr Nádas, retired bank director. He was the organizer of financial aid to those needy Jewish students who had been forced out of domestic universities by the quota

---

* A market town 23 miles north-east of Budapest.

system, and were starving at the universities of Prague, Padua and Paris. The fourth in our row, the lawyer Mr Z., had no knapsack and was lugging a big yellow suitcase. He hung his head and spoke to no one. My head was still aching; I kept straining my neck back, which seemed to help. It would have been a great help to walk with a cane, for the night had worn me down, but back at the sports ground I had given my walking cane to the postal councillor, and it wouldn't do to ask him to return it.

'Close ranks! You too, can't you hear? Why don't you wash your ears?'

Nine o'clock.

Ten.

My headache was all gone. Perhaps I had the fresh air to thank; these medullar headaches could last a day and a half, and powders were usually no help. My waist and thighs felt better too; the marching had helped. And, amazingly, I was no longer tired.

But lest we forget, all this time our brave escort never ceased exhorting us to close ranks, stay in line, step lively. Mostly they used the familiar form of address except for one who was more formal. This was the meanest one, uttering the foulest language regarding our deity and mothers, just like the guard yesterday.

One of the gentlemen ahead, a long-time hiker, turned around to explain how to march efficiently. Head up, breathe through the nose, and no smoking (how convenient; we were not allowed!) and, if possible, no talking. And keep looking at the landscape: it calms the thoughts and refreshes the eyes and the soul.

It was beginning to get warm.

We marched in silence, but occasionally neighbours exchanged a few words. A great, big, silvery pumpkin, glimpsed through the vegetation, received praise. The tall corn also provoked appreciative comments; it was a pleasure to see the sunlight playing on the golden, silky tufts against green leaves. A carriage coming our way was drawn by two white Lippizaners: look at those splendid horses! Even the cows browsing dreamily in the pasture elicited admiration on account of their magnificent sets of lyre-shaped horns.

From the right:

'Close ranks!'

From the left:

'Step lively, you old farts, step lively!'

Behind me, someone sent up a sigh:

'Ah, gentlemen, the times I took the express train to Paris . . .'

Has Anyone Heard of Csomád?

A gentleman ahead of us turned to let us know that we were being taken to Csomád. Supposedly one of the soldiers had let it out of the bag. We passed the news on towards the rear. Murmurs on all sides: Csomád, Csomád, where could it be, and what was it, a hamlet or a large village? Was there a factory there or something?

I had never heard of Csomád.

I hung my head in penance (although this was not the best way to march). I, too, had always been running off to Paris, and in Italy there was no village, no matter how tiny, that I hadn't been curious about. And I had ignored my own homeland. I had never been to Brassó or Kolozsvár; nor to Eger, Nyitra or Pécs. I am forever driven; something calls me to see the world, to visit every last island in the oceans; to see each and every human, all my contemporaries; to caress with my eyes every strange tree, flower, bird. Whereas it should have been my sacred duty to scrutinize my own homeland, and look at each man, woman and child, every grandmother and young girl, to let my eyes take in, as long as I had sight, each horse and each little dog. Now I was atoning for my disloyalty: I had to march and see Csomád.

My inane musings were interrupted by shouts from the rear:

'Doctor! Pass it on!'

'Doctor! Doctor!'

We passed it on.

A doctor turned up soon, carrying his bag. Someone had collapsed.

Of course we kept on marching.

It was getting very hot. Almost like the dog days.

It would have been so fine to rest a little. No one was talking about being thirsty; perhaps if we did not mention it, our thirst would go away.

The doctor was hurrying back to his place. He had given an injection to an old gentleman with heart trouble.

It was past noon.

Our minor torments were beginning to multiply. People were jerking and tugging at their shoulders left and right. The backpack straps were digging in, or slipping off. Those behind tried to help by adjusting the straps for the distressed man in front of them. And every minute you could see, by the bobbing of a head, that someone else had started to limp.

'Close ranks, how many times do I have to tell you!'

'Look lively, pops, or you'll get the rifle-butt!'

'What a dirty rabble, your mother's . . .'

Rest, At Last

At twelve-thirty they let us have half an hour's rest.

We pulled off the road and sank into the weeds on the grassy slope. The wanderers began to masticate. For many (including myself), cigarettes were a priority. Herr Direktor Nádas treated me to some liver pâté; Councillor Aczél gave me biscuits and a shot of cognac; I drank to his health.

The thirty minutes were soon up, short but sweet, and it was a terrific struggle to get up again on feet deadened by the brief rest. The councillor, straightening himself, quoted that oft-heard saying of the poor: 'I wouldn't trade one hundred stand-ups for a single sit-down.' Oh, all the moaning and groaning, and the exasperated laughter in that protracted process of elevating to the vertical: first you lean on your elbows, then palms, then push off with both hands against the ground. Many had fallen asleep and lay there like the dead; these all had to be cruelly tugged awake. Now hundreds were engaged in helping the knapsacks onto the backs of hundreds of others; yesterday after our rest we had found out that it was smarter to help than to watch each other struggle. (For, exhausted as we were, it was excruciating to support the heavy backpack with two arms and then try to get up.)

I was dying of thirst. My neighbours had lukewarm tea in their thermos flasks; now they bitterly regretted not spilling it earlier in the morning to fill them up with fresh cold water. Those who had brains enough to do so were now drinking with great relish, and there was no time to run over and beg a few drops: it was time to fall in.

Afternoon

We were on the go again, marching, marching.

I will forego reciting the ceaseless, monotonous calls for close ranks (interlarded with frequent threats and crude oaths, more frequent than the day before). Our escort continued to maul us until nightfall.

Each step was again painful, just like in the morning. And that enervating, stifling heat. Pouring rain would have been better. Our drovers were all the more infuriated, for they too had to suffer the heat. But the most uncomfortable were those gentlemen who had chosen to wear fur coats for this excursion. I pitied them exceedingly.

Perhaps it was in just such heat that the Jews, laden with even more packs, and also burdened with the sick, feeble old grandmothers, trembling greybeards and little children, had to crawl along when they were expelled from medieval Spain. Also from England, France, Bavaria, Saxony, Württemberg, Austria – everywhere. They had to march through the heat and the storms and the hail, and in freezing cold and dark fog, the way we were marching now.

Doctor!

Ahead of us the column came to a jerky halt, row after row. Some kind of problem up ahead. We halted too; five minutes later we set off again. Then the call came from the rear: Doctor! The doctor hurried back with his bag; another halt. It took another minute or two for him to help out someone who had collapsed. In less than ten minutes, another call for the doctor came from ahead of us. A few minutes later, from the rear. Now the doctor stayed behind; the man whose place he took moved up ahead. On all sides there was much anxiety about what was to come; one had a severe heart condition; another, diabetes; a third, fallen arches; a fourth had recently suffered a gall bladder attack. Herr Direktor N. could barely stay on his feet; in addition to his substantial backpack he was carrying a weighty little suitcase stuffed with food, plus a thick blanket over his arm. I relieved him of the suitcase as my luggage was not too heavy. Councillor A. loaned me his walking cane for a spell. A few minutes later a bony little man of about fifty volunteered to carry the suitcase and the blanket for Herr Direktor N., in return for a bite to eat. He himself carried only a smallish knapsack and no other packs. When N. patted the honest fellow's biceps, the latter said: 'You may rest easy, sir, I used to be a soccer player in my youth, and my legs can take it – I am a waiter by profession.'

So we handed over the little suitcase and the blanket, and walked on, a bit lighter.

A Shot

Again there was a call of 'Doctor! Doctor!' from the rear. We had to pull up. After waiting for a few minutes, we saw the corporal run back to the rear, yelling:

'What the hell's going on with all these lousy Jews?'

After a silence of a minute or two we again heard the corporal:

'You won't stand up? You refuse? I'm going to count. One . . .'

What was going on?

'Two. . .'

Was he going to strike the poor wretch? We saw he had a whip in his hand.

We did not even hear the count of three. A pistol shot rang out. About twenty seconds later, another shot. And then the corporal bawled out:

'Forward march!'

We did not dare to look back, not wanting to see what we would have seen.

The corporal jogged past us, a cigarette dangling from his lips.

A few minutes later the news reached us from the rear. The man who was shot had been a senior railway official, seventy years old, a severe diabetic. He had fainted and the doctor had not been able to revive him. The corporal, after putting two bullets into him, had kicked his body into a ditch.

We marched on in silence.

This was how a life was extinguished now: no announcement, no glass hearse with wreaths, no high-flown funeral orations, no family members in mourning, no old friends around to cast a lump of earth into your grave.

Onward, Onward

It was getting hot, very hot. Everyone was wiping their brow, face, neck. A cart loaded with tiles was creeping alongside our column. Since our guard happened to be out of earshot, someone mustered enough courage to ask the driver:

'How many kilometres to Csomád?'

'Four.'

Four. Well, that wasn't too bad. How strange that walking was more bearable than stopping, which was real torture. If we halted for a minute or two, I began to feel stabbing pains in my feet and legs, the straps cutting into my shoulder; and my back really started to suffer under the relentless pressure of the knapsack. Mr Z., the lawyer, kept shifting that fine pigskin bag from his left hand to his right and back every five minutes. Throughout the afternoon, helping hands kept up the kind adjustment of the backpack straps of the person ahead. By then most of us were marching with heads bared, hat or cap in hand. The fine, verdant landscape, I imagined, should have been a consolation for anyone with a little bit of heart left in his heart. Here and there a solitary ash or elm in the fields; then two lovely white birches standing quite close to each other, like elegant ladies who had stopped for a chat. In the middle distance a line of poplars stood at stiff parade attention for review by the good Lord Himself. Beyond these, in the far distance, a pale hill loomed, trees scattered on its side and bright sunbeams cutting through the sparse woods topping it. A pair of brown butterflies were sparring like boxers nearby. Butterflies, poplars, white birches, cows at pasture: lucky existences, they did not have to be Jews.

Again calls for the doctor began to multiply on all sides. It was half past three. These were people who had, since the murder, somehow mastered their infirmities, and could hold out no longer.

Platoon after platoon, rank after rank pulled up to a halt. Fearful for these unknown comrades who had summoned the doctor, we all stood without a sound, expecting to hear pistol shots any moment. Four doctors, each toting his little bag, had separated from the formation and marched up to the corporal. One of them spoke and then we could hear the corporal shouting something unintelligible at the doctor, over and over. Then all four doctors began talking at the same time, and the corporal had to snap his head from one to the other. At last he turned his back on them and returned to the head of the column. One of the doctors, a greying man, stopped a cart meandering alongside us (one of many) and launched into a palaver with the driver. The cart was loaded with stuffed sacks. Then the doctor walked back to the column. Next, two elderly men were brought out, held by the arms, and another, younger man was carried over, and carefully placed on the cart. Their packs were also fetched; I saw one of the doctors hugging a knapsack belonging to one of the sick men. The cart started off and so did we. For the first minute or two I was aware of the stabbing pains, until my feet became inured again and I marched on, as if not even there. Back in 1914, during the retreat from Serbia (by then I no longer had my horse), I had mastered the art of walking while asleep. Dead tired, hungry and thirsty and sick, I marched hours at a time while asleep, like my companions by my side, on the way to Sabác. All of us 'Chinese' (as the troops made up of remnants of scattered regiments were called) were walking in our sleep, and I still cannot understand how no one toppled over.

One impatient comrade now asked a labourer walking by carrying two beat-up chairs on his back:

'How far is it to Csomád?'

'You're almost there. Hang on!'

Someone in the rear added to this:

'Long live Szálasi!'

We're almost there? Why couldn't we see the church tower? A gentleman turned around to remind us that we had to pass the village of Fót before we came to Csomád.

Fifteen minutes later someone asked a driver on a cart:

'How many kilometres to Csomád?'

'How many? Eight.'

And the other driver had thought it was four.

Ten minutes later we asked another man on a cart crawling past us:

'How many kilometres to Csomád?'

'About five.'

Yet another one, when asked how far, replied: 'Two pipefuls of tobacco.'

After that we did not ask again.

It got to be six o'clock. Twilight was descending.

Again, several men collapsed; we had to stop three or four times within an hour and a half. Our doctors had an idea: the luggage of those older men who were on the verge of collapse was consigned – with the corporal's approval – to loaded carts heading towards Csomád. These carts creaked along almost as slowly as ourselves. Naturally the drivers were to receive money for their services.

We arrived at Fót, site of the Károlyi mansion, a pleasant Baroque structure. As we dragged ourselves past it I sent up another sigh in memory of a former, brighter time, when we had held some military exercises near Fót during the First War. The count invited the entire officers' training corps to a picnic at the mansion. We spent a few charmed hours in the park.

Past Fót, around seven-thirty, we reached a place where the highway split into three branches. Here we were allowed a rest. There was a tavern by the roadside, with some soldiers standing in front. A big, husky, sun-browned lieutenant, about forty-five years old, came out to look at us, and after eyeing us for half a minute, spoke up:

'Is there anything you gentlemen need?'

Hundreds of parched throats answered in unison: 'Water! Water!'

In a minute or two a hefty serving girl came out with two large pitchers of water, followed by the lieutenant carrying eight or ten beer mugs for those who had no cup of their own. That girl had to go back about twenty times to fill those pitchers. Almost everyone gave her a pengő; the poorer ones gave 40 or 60 fillérs.

After glancing around, the lieutenant came up close where the guard could not see him.

'Gentlemen, I feel sorry for you. It is a dirty rotten shame that old men are taken for labour. Believe me, every decent Hungarian is shamefaced at what is being done to the Jews here. It is because of this that Hungary will be wiped off the face of the earth. I am in uniform today because I have a family and I cannot run away from these swine. I happen to know the military commander at Veresegyház, and he is a decent man; I hope he will be able to help you gentlemen. Don't worry, this farce will be over in a few weeks.' He looked around, and added with a little laugh: 'I don't dare to hang around any longer. Rest up, God bless.' He saluted us. 'May the future be better!'

Suddenly he screamed fiercely:

'I want quiet and orderly behaviour here!' (This was for the benefit of an approaching Arrow Cross guard.)

It was time to march on. We forced ourselves into the upright position, and dusted ourselves off. Some were too tired to do that, and left the weeds sticking to their clothes. During our rest the conversation had revolved around the significance of Veresegyház. Yes, on a road sign we now saw the place-name, along with Csomád. Perhaps the labour crew at the latter place belonged under the Veresegyház command. By the way, during the rest stop two of the hikers did not sit down, but remained standing back to back leaning against each other.

I almost forgot: the cart that was carrying luggage for several of the gentlemen had disappeared. It had gone on ahead and vanished. The unfortunate old men were looking up and down the three roads, but no sign of the cart. Their change of clothes, food, blankets, medicines, all they had was gone. They turned from one soldier to another: what were they to do now? Some of the soldiers laughed in their faces at the hopelessness of these complaints.

After this, no one collapsed. The knowledge that we were heading for Veresegyház and would be there within an hour injected a new strength into staggering feet. The heat of the day had let up. It was eveningtime, and to encourage us a few stars appeared. We saw no more carts, only a few straggling pedestrians. Silence reigned in the land, from where the swallows had flown to their African winter grounds. Even the crickets were silent in October, like Gypsy musicians when there are no guests at the tavern. One of our soldier guards started to sing but he was too far away for me to catch his lyrics.

Veresegyház

Around eight we reached the village. At every step we expected a halt, but there was none. We had to march down that long main street while the dogs began to make anti-Semitic noises and shadowy men and women looked on from their doorways at this dark troop of wanderers. We were seized by a terrible despair; each step became pure torment. Where the hell could they be taking us? Had they lied to us again? We had left Veresegyház behind. Not too far off a large hill loomed in the dark. Black trees like SS men stood guard by the roadside.

Finally someone ahead of us turned back with the news: we were headed for Erdőváros, three kilometres away, just around that hill.

Our steps became a bit livelier. At least we could see our destination. Dr Z. kept switching his suitcase from his hand to his shoulder and back. Since the noontime rest he had been lugging the suitcase alternately on his left and right shoulder; easier to carry that way, but hard on the arm supporting it. He said he had always felt sorry for the porters at train stations who carried heavy luggage from the train to the taxi.

We still had to stagger across the small community of Erdőváros before we reached a long stretch of fence topped by barbed wire. Behind it lay a giant, prison-like building. This was the brick factory, the vague outline of its dark smokestack stabbing at the sky. We stood and stood in front of that barbed-wire fence, God only knows why. We stood there for ten years. (Or even longer: for a whole half an hour!) Then came the shouting from up front; they started to herd us in. We had to march two by two across a plank over a ditch. You may imagine how long that took. Soldiers with fixed bayonets were strolling on the factory grounds. It was a pretty big spread of land, with the shadow of a building here and there. Again line up by fours. And there we stood inside: it was 9 p.m.

At Night

There was a stir at the head of the line. Some of the men, probably the younger ones, went running off; what was this all about? We soon found out: they were sent to bring straw.

Ten, twenty, thirty men were soon carrying armloads of straw towards one corner of that giant building. Around ten we all had to march to the other end of the building where a broad plank with a railing led up to the loft. We barrelled into that long and dark loft like so many sheep into a barn. A few candles flickered their red light in the darkness, while straw rustled on all sides. We were going to sleep on straw. I soon lost my marching companions as we stumbled around in the dark. All told there must have been a thousand of us up there. A hellish pandemonium reigned (although who knows if the damned make that much noise in hell . . .). Everyone was look-ing for a place, everyone was forging ahead, everyone was shouting the names of good chums. Howls of pain for every corn and bunion trod upon, moans and curses where some-one fell and was trampled. Cries of help came from at least six places where people fell into ventilation holes that had been left uncovered. I must have fallen down three or four times before somehow making my way to the other end of the loft. There near the wall I dropped into a narrow spot that was unoccupied, pulled off my knapsack and placed it under my head. The straw, alas, was strewn in a very thin layer on the brick floor. On the ledge nearby one lonely candle was burn-ing. In its light I recognized someone who had bunked down near me: Dr Bálint, attorney for the Journalists' Association. My other neighbours were unknown to me.

An actor friend of mine used to tell an anecdote from his

youth when, performing in a provincial town, he and five others were quartered at a widow's house, and bunked on a bed of boards, without any bedding.

'Well, sir, those boards were so hard that every five minutes I had to get up and rest.'

Well, these bricks weren't any better. I tried putting my blanket under me, but five minutes later I was too cold. Since it wasn't much help underneath, I pulled the blanket over me.

The notion of eating had not even occurred to me. And, wonder of wonders, I did not miss smoking either. Sleep, only sleep mattered. But it took from ten to midnight for everyone to find a place, and to leave passageways to the exit on both sides.

This night promised to be worse than the one before. Complaints and arguments raged unrestrained. Those lying across from me were squeezed over; two feet were laid across my thigh, a third foot descended on my left shoulder. We held council to create some order; I pulled back as far as I could and bent my legs, but it was not much better. My two neighbours opposite me did what they could; at last we arrived at a solution: I overlapped one leg between my neighbour's and laid the other by his side. Similar arrangements were made by other neighbouring parties. I placed my hat on my belly. There was no question of taking off our clothes. From the entrance a soldier screamed at us: 'Lights out!' It became pitch-black. The straw kept rustling in the dark. And each moment moans and curses, and nasty hacking and hawking. A few snores, even, from the happy ones who could sleep. The soles of my feet and my entire nervous system were burning. I carried on a languishing conversation with Dr Bálint until 1 a.m. and then fell asleep, in spite of the hard bricks, the noise and the cold.

Sunday

I was resurrected around eight in the morning. Dr Bálint was already awake but still lying down. He too felt like his body had been crushed in a mortar. He told me that he had woken in the middle of the night to relieve his bladder, and had had to roam around for half an hour, stumbling in the dark, before reaching the exit. When he had stepped outside a soldier had yelled at him and pointed his rifle, thinking that here was a Jew trying to escape. It had been hard enough to persuade the man to let him out. (Others had had the same experience that night.) On the way back it had taken Dr Bálint another half-hour to reach his place, after stepping on a hundred feet and bellies, and falling down about fifty times.

By the time we went down in the morning almost the entire troop was assembled, standing about in flocks like penguins. There were smaller groups of six and seven here and there in the large open space and, further down, another crowd 800- or 1,000-strong. They were quartered in a long, single-storey building. Most were done with washing and breakfast; many were smoking cigarettes, cigars, pipes. We found out there was a well nearby, behind a warehouse. We poured buckets of water into the long, low, tin trough and washed ourselves down to our ankles, brushed our teeth, combed our hair. Across from the warehouse lay a small white building, the office. Grim buildings were scattered all over the place, as well as gigantic piles of bricks. We had slept in the drying loft. In front of it were strolling militiamen armed with obsolete rifles, and a few younger soldiers of the regular army. I learned that soldiers here, both old and young, were called *keret* (cadres). Men were circulating in between the crowd and various groups, turning their heads in all directions and shouting names. Dr Bálint and I squatted down by the wall of the warehouse, where some grass grew. I accepted a bite of cheese from him and offered some fruit jam in return. Then we went to take back our heavy knapsacks. On the way I was intercepted by Herr Direktor Nádas; he came up with us to show me where he bunked near a pillar, and invited me to join them. I thanked him, but stayed where I was by the wall. I did not have the heart to leave Dr Bálint behind. Our physicians were accosted by hundreds of men in the courtyard reciting a thousand complaints. But there was nothing to be done, without any beds or medication. When I went down again, every minute some person would come up to introduce himself. One gentleman went as far as to quote one of my poems: too bad it was written by someone else. Another claimed that he had nearly died laughing at one of my *croquis*. (Me too: the piece he referred to was one of Karinthy's most brilliant sketches.[*]) For the first five or six days there was a constant stream of these introductions; good heavens, now I would have to say hello to all these folks as long as I lived.

So we stood around or sat on small piles of bricks, all morning long.

---

[*] Karinthy, Frigyes (1887–1938), humourist, playwright, poet.

A Relative

Around ten a forced labourer with a white armband, accompanied by a young soldier, came up to me.

The labourer said: 'Pardon me, sir, I am V., a forced labourer, and this soldier would like to talk to you.'

The soldier clicked his heels together.

'With all due respect, we are related. My name is Péter Pál Szép. I just heard that you were here, uncle, and I thought I'd come and pay my respects.'

And he held out his hand, with affection in his eyes.

'Son, we cannot be related, I am Jewish.'

'Makes no difference!'

'That's mighty brave of you to think that way, dear Péter, or do they call you Pál?'

'Pete.'

'Well, dear Pete then, we are namesakes, but that's no big thing. But if it makes you feel good, we can be pals.'

'But we are related!' he insisted, almost angry.

We had an audience by now, smiling gentlemen who patted Pete and bestowed friendly squeezes.

The upshot was, Pete respectfully inquired if I smoked, and pulled out a tin case. He replaced it mournfully and made me promise to send for him if I needed anything. He was serving with the forced labourers, in a nearby compound.

At noon, after I had had a bite of bread and jam, Pete turned up again. With a mess tin.

'I had to look for you all over the place, uncle. Please accept this potato soup. It's tasty.'I had to accept. There was enough to share with three other gentlemen. They had spoons, I didn't.

A little later, after I had sat down by a pile of bricks, a

thin, blond forced labourer stepped up to me. He was Albert
Havas, correspondent to English and American newspapers.
Did I need anything? One after another, that same day, he
brought me a mess tin, a spoon, a brand-new cherry wood cigarette holder and cigarette paper, which was in short supply.

Around three in the afternoon another forced labourer,
a good-looking young man, stood in front of me to introduce
himself: Dr K., working in the office. The captain had request-
ed me to come in for a visit. Everyone was glad to hear this: it
could only mean good news for us all.

Captain Megay

There were four forced labourers assigned for office
duty: Dr K. (a young lawyer), an art student, an actor and a
philosopher. I found out that all kinds of work – welding of
broken rails, hewing of railway ties, blacksmith work – was
done at the brick factory, except brick manufacture. I knocked
on the door of the captain's room. Inside, the radio was blaring
front-line reports. As I entered the captain raised his head; he
had been leaning on his fists, scrutinizing the map. The captain had a human face. He must have been about thirty-two.

'Captain Megay.'

He turned off the radio.

I was to excuse him for making me take the trouble. Did
I prefer Symphony cigarettes or his hand-rolled ones? He had
been very much looking forward to meeting me. He himself
could not come out; he was not free to visit with us. He lived
with his family here at the compound, but he could not ask me

for dinner. His only contact with us was providing shelter at the factory. In any case he had ordered the guards to act as humanely as possible. He had had the straw brought in. He wished he could do something about our food; he would make every effort. The Arrow Cross command was at Csomád, and we belonged to them. They disapproved of him, and considered him a Jew-lover.

After that, I had small hope when I asked the captain if he could do something about letting the men over sixty, brought here against regulations, go home. At least the oldest ones, and the invalids. No, he was very sorry, there was nothing he could do, except maybe get himself transferred, with worse consequences for us.

We conversed for a little while longer; the captain was very much interested in literature and read as much as his time allowed. Finally he encouraged me to call on him if I needed anything.

I could see he was visibly relieved when I said goodbye. At any moment one of the Arrow Cross people could have walked in.

On the way out, the armed militiaman with the straw-blond moustache, whom I had seen on the way in, turned to me:

'Excuse me, aren't you Mr Ernő Szép?'

I said I was.

'I thought I recognized you when you went in, but I didn't believe it was possible.'

'Where do you know me from?'

'From *Tolnai Világlap*,* where I have seen your picture many times. I've read so many fine stories from your pen.'

Fine stories.

* An illustrated weekly.

It turned out he was a local cooper. I would have taken him for a farmer. He was fifty years old and had a grandson already. His son was at the front. He had been wasting his time in this uniform for a year and a half now. Would to God we were rid of these bandit Germans. In the First War, too, he would have liked to kill those Germans; if it weren't for them, this country would have been just fine.

People sat or stood or loitered around in the compound. In the middle of a small circle of men someone was reading aloud from a *Pesti Hírlap*.* (It had been brought by one of the forced labourers.)

I heard that a lance corporal wearing an Arrow Cross armband had been there to give a speech. He said we had been given a day off not because it was Sunday, but because the equipment was not ready. Next morning we would start. He ordered an engineer to read aloud a sheet of typed text. It contained the work schedule, and punishments for sabotage, disobedience or attempted escape (beating, hanging head down from a tree, execution). Reveille at four-thirty, ready to march at six.

A corporal of the guard had announced that anyone trying to go past the barbed wire would be shot. He also warned that the ground within two metres of the fence was mined. (This turned out to be a lie.)

Dr Bálint and I walked past the smokestack. We reached a vast, square yard flanked by two perpendicular rows of whitewashed houses, like servants' quarters on an estate. The third side of the yard had the drying loft and a huge, tile-roofed shed, and four or five buildings of various sizes, the workshops. The fourth side was open field. Everywhere Jewish, Romanian and Serbian forced labourers were at work. In one

* A Budapest daily.

workshop they were filing iron, from another came the hiss of welding. Trolleys on a narrow gauge were pushed from the shed amid sounds of 'Hi hi!' and 'Prr prr!' – these were the Romanians and Serbs. Past the drying loft we discovered another yard surrounded by buildings. Half the yard was over-run by weeds, the other half was cultivated. Among the buildings and workers stood armed guards.

We Are Going to Dig Trenches

Back in our area a huge crowd was abuzz with the news: some forced labourers had let it be known that we were going to be employed at the earthworks, which meant digging trenches. This is what had caused the hubbub. Not one among all these creased trousers had ever dug trenches before.

Dr Bálint gave me a bemused smile. He was a thin, fair-haired man with thick glasses, soft-spoken, his face still like a student's. Certain adults retain their boyish features to a surprising degree. Dr Bálint was 52 and had a weak heart. How was he going to survive digging trenches? I did not worry about myself; I would see the following day. For the time being each and every bone in my body was aching from the night before and our two days' march.

We were ordered up to the loft by six. Lighting candles was forbidden. The loft had small, square, latticed ventilation windows, promising some light while twilight lingered. I still had a piece of bread and plenty of jam; I could ration the bread for the night and the morning, and by noon we should get something to eat.

Again we positioned ourselves along the side walls, where I had left my blanket and knapsack. We sat for a while, thinking with dismay about having to sleep on that cold brick floor again. The straw had a nauseating smell. Fresh straw has a pleasant scent, but this was tired old straw. I remembered this miserable straw smell from my student years; it was what my straw mattresses used to exhale back then. Now it was my turn to show interest in the neighbours. Sitting and eating on my left was Mr Stein, the traveller; not the Asia-traveller Aurel Stein, but a domestic travelling salesman. But he had not travelled for years, even here at home; the law required that travelling salesmen had to be Aryans. Another neighbour across from me, Mr D., with whom my legs were in such intimacy, had been in insurance, and the other, Mr M., was a commission agent. (I tactfully did not inquire what kind.) The first thing Mr Stein wanted to know, right after we had introduced ourselves, was whether we had heard rats or mice running around the night before. He wasn't sure if he had heard any, God forbid; possibly he had hallucinated them, but he couldn't sleep a wink all night.

'Gentlemen, if you had any idea of the hotels I had to sleep in, you'd understand why I am a nervous wreck.'

God only knows what these men who had been deprived of their livelihood had been living on. The poor and elderly among them could not support themselves with physical labour. I know that among the Jewish suicides of these years there were many who took their lives in desperate poverty.

The guests at the 'Hôtel des Tuileries' (the name some wag gave the brick factory on the first day) had discovered that candles could be lit as long as the ventilation windows were covered with shirts and dark jackets. So the candles were lit. Many had brought candles; that was very smart. Again the noise rivalled the night before. People shifted about, there was not enough room for body and baggage, so others' bags were moved, shoved aside. Some picked themselves up and tried to move near friends, treading on hands, heads and feet, tripping again and again in the process; in the end they had to make the return journey, if there was not enough room near the friend. In the afternoon a group of men had come up here to create rows, some semblance of order, but there was simply not enough room. Now there were hisses and shouts calling for quiet. Oh, how ugly and mean it all was!

Alas, there were many coarse characters among us. More and more voices were yelling and screaming for silence, creating more disturbance than the original noise itself.

By the time the uproar died down, the snoring had set in: snorts and asthmatic coughs hacked away at one's eardrums. Some of these coughs were like mountainsides crumbling after an explosion.

Boring, isn't it? And how.

To top it all, smoking was prohibited. That was going to be a tough one to get used to.

All of a sudden, from the other end:

'Doctor! Doctor!'

Ten, twenty voices passed on the call.

Then it was quiet again.

Some ten minutes later we in the back learned that the doctor had been called for an old gentleman with diabetes, who had collapsed on the march several times.

About five minutes later, loud shouts came from that corner: 'Be quiet! Silence! Won't you shut up!' (This last hoarse voice was the angriest.)

The whispering grapevine revealed that the old gentleman had started to moan: 'I am dying, gentlemen, I'm dying; you'll see, I'm going to die.' This was why he was shouted down so rudely by those who wanted to sleep. (The old man was not exaggerating; he died around midnight.)

The doctor had to struggle over to four or five other invalids. Heart, gall bladder, asthma. Occasionally the din died down, only to flare up again in twenty places at once.

I would not have been able to sleep, but I so very much wanted to rest. But that merciless, hard brick floor . . . I would lie on my back, say, for three minutes, then I had to turn on my side. Then the back again, then the other side. Then I lay on my stomach. In every position I tried to tenderly swaddle myself in the blanket. Dr Bálint was doing the same, and we exchanged a chuckle or two in our pain. Of course both of us kept apologizing to the neighbours who were caused discomfort by these changes of position.

The candles were put out one after another, and the clothes hung over the windows were removed. Lying on my back, I glued my eyes on a window, in the hope of a little moonlight. Both of my feet were killing me, throbbing in protest of the fact that for the third night in a row my socks and shoes stayed on. Otherwise my feet would have been too cold. Mr Stein complained of heartburn, even though all he had had to eat was bread and cheese. For a while longer I kept hearing sighs, growls, coughs, snorts, squabbles, then miraculously I drifted off.

Morning

'*Auf! Auf! Auf!*' Pitch-dark, 4.30 a.m. We had no alarm clocks; I don't know who woke us, who was the first to wake exactly at four-thirty. Me, even if I had to travel, or show up in court, I was unable to get up on time. Especially that early. All my life I had enormous respect for people who told me they could get up exactly when they wanted to. That had to be sheer genius. I was amazed such genius was never apparent at first glance. But then Leo Tolstoy did not look like a genius either.

By the time I was done with the first cigarette and had washed and had breakfast (we had to stand in line at the well), momentous events had transpired at the compound.

We had been divided into companies, and the companies into platoons. Two hundred and forty men in a company, sixty in a platoon. Now our names were being taken for the lists. This was accomplished at a table where six engineers were seated; the table and chairs had been brought from the office. Our engineers sported round white badges with red circles on their lapels; doctors had the same, with red crosses. The office must have provided these as well.

Because of the general hubbub we all had to shout our name, age, Budapest address. One company was already gathered and lined up. The names were dictated row by row.

The engineers were to be our overseers.

Each of the doctors was surrounded by a pushing, shoving mob. The doctors kept throwing up their arms and shouting in exasperation:

'Impossible, I am sorry, impossible, gentlemen; I cannot do anything. Please, gentlemen, understand, it's impossible.'

Many were shaving near the brick piles, having placed their kits on top of the bricks. Others bent over to apply shoepaste. I had meant to do that myself, but my sister in her hurry had given me black shoepaste, and I was wearing yellow boots.

The Artist

I was suddenly accosted by a lanky, aristocratic-looking, heavily unshaven person wearing a soldier's cap, a beat-up trench coat and a white armband. He sported long 'artist's hair', such as no self-respecting artist wears, hanging from under his cap.

'Hello there, I was looking for you all day yesterday!'

He introduced himself as Steve something-or-other, a painter, claimed we had known each other from long ago at the Fészek Club,* and were together at several art openings and picnics; oh, what charming times those were.

He had been serving as a forced labourer, but was let go because of his shaky mental condition. He had been baptized at birth; only one of his parents was Jewish. And still, they had dragged him off now, what unheard-of swinishness.

And, he went on to relate, the day before yesterday he lost his knapsack on the road at the rest stop. All of his tobacco was in it. For God's sake, could he bum a cigarette off me. Many thanks.

Shovel, Spade

After we had all given our names and addresses, a new company was formed, and I was assigned to the second platoon. We were called 92/2. Why 92? Someone thought it was the number of labour companies scattered throughout the

* Artists', actors' and writers' club in Budapest, still extant.

region. Herr Direktor Nádas again discovered me and I was obliged to stand next to him in formation.

At the gate, two large army wagons awaited us, jam-packed with our tools. These were unloaded amid much clatter: spades, shovels, pickaxes.

We marched over by platoons, everyone taking a spade or shovel. Pickaxes were only for the younger, more vigorous ones. These instructions were roared out by our company commander, a strapping engineer about forty-six or forty-eight. After all of us were thus armed and we were lined up again (we had another engineer as our platoon commander), our company commander stood up on a brick pile and gave a most captain-like speech.

He had a commanding, handsome, clean-shaven and virile face, and a hawk's nose. He wore a hunting hat, and a long, yellow leather coat over a sports coat.

'First of all, we are not misters here, but comrades, so let's use the informal mode of address. (Several people cheered.) We are living dramatic times, so let us act in a comradely manner towards each other, each for all; do whatever can be done. We are to keep order and discipline. Whoever goes against orders will first of all have to face me. We must do our work in a manner befitting our honour and best interest. We survived the march here, and we shall put up with the work as well. Most of us after all have fought through the First War, so let us think of those hardships to find strength for our current trials. Shoulder your tools, and forward, comrades!'

All the feeble, old, sick men around me listened to this rousing speech with heads hung low.

Our company commander hurried to the fore and we heard his soldierly command:

'Form straight lines! Close ranks! Step lively!'

And out we went through the gate, straight down the

single street of Erdőváros, lined by neat, little tile-roofed houses. It was six in the morning, and we hardly saw any sign of
life. We headed for Veresegyház, passing a train station on the
way. We marched through Veresegyház. How much farther?
We had another three kilometres to go. I was hurting all over,
carrying that beautiful brand-new spade, like a recruit his
weapon. I had left the shovels for the older ones. Our rows
became more and more crooked; it was a mercy we had no
guards to yell at us.

Past the village on the left there was a small forest and a
cemetery. It was a peaceful scene to behold. Faded white and
rose headstones among the wooden crosses. And on the right,
a little way down, waiting for us on the sunlit grass was a
small group of men, part uniformed, part civilian, all wearing
armbands. And the earthworks were visible, for this was
where they began, and ran for a distance of three or four hundred metres.

A Small Surprise

Out of that group one corporal advanced towards us,
screamed 'Halt!' and waved over the commander of the company ahead of us. The Jewish commander stood at attention
listening to the corporal for a few minutes, then returned and
sent a man running to our group. What was up? Well, we
were to surrender all our valuables: watches, rings, any gold
or silver objects we had with us. We also had to give up flashlights, cigarette lighters, fountain pens. Whoever hid anything
would be shot.

A civilian boy and a soldier came our way carrying a

large basket, and began to collect the goods and place them carefully into it. When they reached us in less than half an hour, a trembling, white-haired man three rows ahead dared to speak up:

'Gentlemen, I have worn this wedding ring for forty-five years, it's my only keepsake from my poor dead wife, for God's sake.'

'Shut up!'

Some rings were hard to take off, and the gentlemen let out nervous groans. Trouser and waistcoat pockets yielded up their gold pens and fine silver cigarette cases, the owners hastily having removed the cigarettes. Many flashlights came out of hiding; after all some had dared to hold on to them back at the racecourse. Silence reigned; no one expressed indignation, as we stood there fleeced (I had nothing to give, having left even my watch at home); at most I heard muttered comments such as: 'What can you say? My God, if I had only known. That fine Patek watch. We were pretty stupid not to think of this.'

After an hour they lugged the basket away, and we could march on, all the way to the unfinished earthworks. We had to advance to the grassy area where four or five youths awaited us, one civilian among them in black, complete with boots, armband and an unusually large holster.

Now we had to hand over our money.

Two beat-up suitcases gaped in front of a soldier seated on a stool. On his knees he balanced some kind of folder.

It took an awfully long time to hand over the money, because the seated soldier wrote down everyone's name and Budapest address. The youth with the armband reassured our company commander that our money would be returned in Budapest, and our valuables would be given back when we left here. I handed over my one and only 100-pengő note. I hadn't brought any more, thinking what did we need money for. Some surrendered 1,500, 3,000 and more. One man, I later heard, handed over 15,000. He brought all that money hoping it would buy his freedom. I almost forgot: everyone could keep ten pengős in small change. On the way to the two suitcases, there was a flurry of money-changing; extra coins were passed around to those who lacked the ten. Meanwhile soldiers and Arrow Cross men sidled up to us:

'Pops, why don't you pass me a hundred, you'll never get it back anyway. Just stick it in my palm.'

There were some who were scared, and gave. There were some who were scared but did not give. (Afraid to be caught.) The soldiers whispered in the non-givers' ears:

'Just you wait, filthy Jew. Just you wait.'

After the money had been taken, the civilian with the armband (a youth with a vile, ugly face) gave everyone a body search. He dug out every wallet and every pocket, stuck his finger into shoes above the ankle, and groped over plus-fours.

It must have been around eleven when these proceedings were over.

Now we were led back to the unfinished earthworks.

Coats had to be placed on the grass. (Many wore winter overcoats.) A few dozen gentlemen had even brought their knapsacks. Across from us, at the end of the earthworks, stood a civilian we had not seen before, in the company of a corporal and a few soldiers. He held a long, wooden triangle, and a round, copper case from which a string dangled. The corporal ordered all of the engineers over, and the civilian began to hold forth to them. He was an ordinary man with a gentle face, and his voice was also gentle. He explained that the ditch had to be three metres wide and three metres deep, and one metre wide at the bottom. Our engineers were expected to be able to comply with these measurements.

Endre Frank

When the civilian surveyor reached this point, a soldier came up to us, and making a megaphone out of his hands, yelled:

'Endre Frank! Move it!'

A young man, wearing grey plus-fours, who stood among our engineers, turned around and ran towards the soldier. His face showed how startled he was, hearing his name called out. I knew him. When we stopped near Csomád to rest, he brought me a glass of water. I thanked him for this unexpected kindness, and shook hands with him. He introduced himself: Endre Frank, architect. Up till now he had been allowed to stay in Budapest, where he worked on renovating army barracks. He was 36 years old and married. He looked like a delicate, fair-skinned Japanese with blue eyes. Here at Erdőváros we had had a chance to talk a little bit. He was a voracious reader with a well-developed, courageous critical sense. Now he too was enlisted among our engineers and wore the badge with the red circle.

Well, Endre Frank rushed off, while we had to pay attention to the work assignments handed out to us. First of all about twenty men with spades began marking the straight lines on each side within which we were supposed to excavate. We heard a dull pop from the direction where our money had been taken away. Hardly anyone looked up. But then another soldier came running, shouting for a doctor. What could it have been? But our work had already commenced. We had to line up, one after another, platoon by platoon, along the marked lines on two sides and start digging. The earth had to be thrown behind, where the older ones, who were standing by, would shovel it away. Most of the men digging were seized by a certain youthful ardour. The earthworks fascinated them; it seemed a welcome change after the boredom and melancholy of standing around. The engineers went from man to man down the line (they and the doctors were exempt from labour) and advised everyone not to attack the spade with such eagerness, that would only make the soles of our shoes slip off. The spade had to be sunk into the soil with patience. Reaching a rocky spot, one of the engineers called for a man with a pickaxe. The soldiers walked about in silence behind our backs, carrying sticks they had cut from trees. All around there were green trees, blooming with life. Someone near me remarked that it was strange that the engineer Frank had not returned yet. They couldn't have . . .

A minute later the doctor trudged back with head hung low. He sent four younger men with spades back where he came from.

Fifteen minutes later all of us knew that Endre Frank had been shot in the head by that Arrow Cross thug. The four men with spades had been ordered to dig his grave.

One of the guards yelled at us:

'Shut your mouths! No yapping during work!'

Now even the flurry of excited whispering died off. We were all left to wonder in silence about the reason for this tragedy.

You may imagine our mood.

Periodically some of our guards stopped for a little chat among themselves. They glanced in our direction and chuckled.

Slowly the two lines with spades moved on. Once or twice the surveyor took the spade out of someone's hand to demonstrate the proper technique. Then it was my turn for a lesson. I was curious to see how I would take to the labour. I had tried spadework before, not only as a child, but also in my student days when I worked as a tutor on the *puszta*, the Great

Plain. I had not been able to put up with it for long; my back would soon start to hurt. I had also wanted to try mowing with a scythe; the movements were so beautiful, pure dance. Well, that made my hands ache for days. So now I began to dig. It felt good. Ever since the decrees against Jews I had not played tennis, my only exercise being calisthenics each morning. It would be refreshing now to try out my muscles again. Digging felt good for my stiff body, still sore from the hard bedding. But I had lost some weight and grown weaker since the German takeover in March. Yet, strange to say, I felt more powerful than as a 17-year-old back on the *puszta*. I made an effort to dig as evenly as the surveyor showed me. The question was, how long would I be able to keep it up? I had not anticipated so much resistance from the sandy soil. It had not rained here for some time.

Lunchtime Minus Lunch

We were all digging now, in two long lines. Every minute someone straightened up to massage his waist or back. People stole a quick glance left and right, for the guards stood close behind the lines ready to chastise anyone trying to take a rest. My neighbours were wiping the sweat from foreheads, panting, sighing, looking in all directions for succour. There were glances sent up heavenwards; perhaps the Almighty would intervene and forbid the digging of trenches. Everyone was digging, the scrawny and the bent, people with unspeakably tired faces, and the fat ones, too, whose paunches made bending most difficult. I couldn't tell whose lot was harder.

Our guards began to encourage us more and more frequently:
'Push, don't hold back!'
'Faster, work faster!'
'What's the matter, pops, you fall asleep?'
'Let's go, or you'll get a beating!'
Suddenly a corporal was coming down the line, shouting:
'Lunchtime! Half an hour! Lunch is on the way!'

It must have been around twelve-thirty; we had no watches. That is, we had one: they let our company commander keep his.

The crew scattered.

We at once surrounded the doctor who had been ordered back, and he told us that poor Endre Frank had been shot for hiding 70 pengős in his plus-fours. An engineer who had stood next in line to Frank verified the amount. As Frank was walking away after he had been searched and his name written down, the Arrow Cross man noticed a ten-pengő bill sticking out from the bottom of his plus-fours. They let him pass, until they were finished with the rest of the company. And then . . .

We scattered over the grass in silent, tired groups; twenty men here, four or five there, and there were some who sat solitary, far from others. We were all waiting for lunch, wondering what they would give us. All eyes were directed towards the village, where our food had to come from. But it did not come. The few who had brought some food with them began to dig it up, but it wasn't much. I had pocketed a fistful of jam, a light meal. After much searching I found my overcoat. I also took out my gloves since the handle of the spade had started to give me blisters.

I camped out next to a dear old friend I had just discovered here: Mihály Pásztor, who had written so many interesting items about Budapest in the *Pesti Napló* of the good old peacetime, and later in *Magyar Hírlap*.* He was 69 years old, suffering from diabetes, and had no news from his only son. I offered him and two other neighbours some jam. Poor Mihály Pásztor was one of those whose belongings had been stolen by a carter on the march here. While we sat there the sponging artist spotted us and greeted me effusively. He wanted food and a cigarette. There was a mouthful of jam left, and he got his smoke; there was no bread to offer, alas.

Some good folks spread the word there was water to be had, a small stream flowing behind some trees. We thronged towards the water, which was indeed good to drink and cool. Most of us used the palm of our hands. According to a Greek sage whose name escapes me, the most regal drink is that out of your palm. (As the hart panteth after water . . .)

We rested a little longer than half an hour. The surveyor, that quiet, decent man, walked among us and inquired about how we were getting on, who was hurting where. 'This work is not for the likes of you,' he said to a one-eyed old man, 'and whoever assigned you to this did not know what earthworks are all about. And what's the use of it, anyhow? Well, I'll say no more; these days no Hungarian is free to speak in plain language.'

He had a nail missing on one hand, and gave his attention to the scab on that finger. He told us we were to work until five. There were about 1,600 men digging and our workload was 5,000 cubic metres a day. Wishing us strength and endurance, he walked on. I caught a glimpse of Steve, our friend the artist, munching something else now and smoking with another group.

Our guards were approaching; groan, we had to stand up. What if lunch were to be brought after all? Maybe they

* Budapest dailies before and after World War I.

would let us bolt it down. We were all starving.

And we dug on. I had already noted certain gentlemen who, as soon as the guards walked past, stopped digging and leaned on their spades and looked on as the rest worked. Our engineers had already designated the oldest among us as shovellers (who had remained idle so far), to stand behind the diggers and shovel the excavated earth further back. The surveyor began to circulate among these now, and instructed them, demonstrating for each, how to stand up straight, hold the handle like this, not too low, slide it under the clods and swing it away so they fell at a distance. Meanwhile, the soldiers came and went, bawling out people; this became a constant refrain, just as on the march, but the lyrics were different:

'Push that spade, harder, harder!'

'Move it, move it!'

'They're all asleep!'

'Load up that shovel!'

'What's this, sabotage?'

The loudest was a corporal with a face like a red onion, and he had a stick, with which he hit people from behind, or else smashed them in the back with his fist so they went flying. After an hour's digging, the work began to get more and more painful, especially because of the hunger pangs. My only nourishment was to look up at the sky; it was so beautifully spring-like and full of violets up there. I was afraid that they would reprimand me because of my gloves. About fifty paces away an old man toppled over; the shovel dropped from his hands. The doctor came and had him taken back a way, to lie on the grass. Two soldiers started yelling about this, but let go after a while. Several others who collapsed that afternoon were likewise given a rest. It occurred to me that I did not know when and how the man who died the night before had been buried. Looking at the oldest and sickest around me, I thought: how many would last until they sent us home?

We struggled on all afternoon. (Lunch never did arrive.)

When we were ordered to fall into formation at five it took me a while to find my coat, buried under a pile of others. We shouldered our spades and lined up by fours. Our company commander, the engineer Gyula Marton, a dreamy, gentle man, did not know how to shout orders. Before we marched off, the corporal, Red Onion, yelled to remind us that tomorrow we were to leave at a quarter to six, because we had arrived late today. And whoever had any valuables back at quarters better hand it over, because tomorrow there would be a search of our knapsacks, and whoever was hiding anything would be shot.

Helping arms supporting our ailing comrades, we marched off. Fortunately we were not required to sing.

A Warm Spoon

Back in front of the office there stood a forced labourer waiting for us, roaring at the top of his voice: 'Dinner's here!' We were to march, lined up by platoons, around the drying shed.

Everyone ran to clamber up to the loft for mess tins and spoons.

In that back yard that was part weeds and part vegetable garden three or four giant kettles awaited us. Two Serb prisoners ladled out dinner for us. Those who had already been served came past with the news: bean soup for dinner. And, as they were swallowing it: 'It's burnt!'

Although the aroma was not very appetizing, I ate up those beans as fast as I could. Even the most weak-stomached among us spooned it all up. By seven we had all had our dinner, and took our tins and spoons to wash at the well. And then the obligatory cigarette, of course.

As we went up to the loft someone found the torn pieces of a 100-pengő note. The explanation was easy: whoever had hidden it in the morning got scared, and was mean enough to tear it up, rather than give it to some poor forced labourer: Jew, Serb or Romanian.

Hebrew Melody and Tears

As soon as we were all in place up there, a loud voice asked for silence. When he got what he asked for, he announced that there would be a memorial service for our poor comrade, Endre Frank.

At this everyone grew hushed; even the last whispered squabbles died off.

After a minute's silence someone in the middle of the floor began to say a Hebrew prayer in a fine, loud baritone. And back here, too, those who knew the prayer began to murmur and whisper along. The whole loft was humming. Of course we were all standing. Five minutes later the prayer was over, and the same strong, pleasing baritone launched into a chant. (He was the cantor of one of the Budapest temples.) On hearing the heart-rending, mournful melody many of us started to sniffle. Those who were familiar with the chant sang along softly, but many broke into sobs. The cantor, carried away by fervour and ambition, sang louder and louder, until, bang-bang, two shots were fired down below. No one was hit; the bullets went through the roof. The warrior on guard must have imagined the Jews were having too good a time. After this gentle warning the cantor lowered his voice.

When the chant ended the usual squabbles broke out. Someone had been kicked, someone's boots were in the way; someone took up more space than was his by rights; someone dropped or spilled something over someone else. There were two rows of pillars supporting the roof and these had a ledge running around them on which people placed their cups, candles, food, tins, spoons, shoehorns, collars, ties, eyeglasses, false teeth and whatnot. People were constantly kneeling up and rummaging on this ledge. Insults came flying from all corners:

'Idiot, can't you take care!'

'Ah, the boorishness one has to put up with!'

'Shut your mouth!'

'Who were you going to slap, you ugly Jew!'

I pity people not when they weep but when they quarrel. The comradely courtesies that we had been called on to observe, as you may see, had been forgotten. There were many ordinary types, the louder ones, and seedy-looking characters as well, who delighted in addressing those richer and better-dressed in casual, informal language, while these latter gentlemen remained reserved, for the most. I must confess to not being ready to hobnob with everyone; it took eight or ten days to politely discourage those comrades who forced their attentions on me.

As for the loudmouths, our company and platoon

commanders threatened in vain to report them – it went like this each night. And what was worse, even in the middle of the night there would be loud outbursts when those who had to relieve themselves stumbled in the narrow passageways and fell or stepped on sleepers. In view of all the straw, candles were strictly forbidden, and still, here and there, candles were lit on the ledges. What's more, a few desperate smokers lit one up whenever they thought everyone was asleep. Terrible outbursts would rage then:

'Put out that cigarette, you scoundrel!'

'Who dares to smoke with all this straw around? Hit him!'

'He belongs in a madhouse!'

'Who are you, cowardly scum!'

'Tear him apart! Lynch him!'

The smoker would lie low, hiding the burning cigarette in his hand; some took a furtive drag even as the storm raged. This went on every night. It is a miracle that the loft did not burn down with all of us in it.

Oh, yes: Dr Lukács, who lay near me and saw my inadequate blanket, gave me the camel-hair blanket that had belonged to Endre Frank.

The Second Day

My whole body was one big mass of cramps at dawn when my neighbours roused me from my dreams. Dr Bálint and Mr Stein helped me to my feet. (They too could have used some help.) Everybody was hurting from yesterday's sport. There is only one remedy against bodily misery of this type, as

I had found out in my youth (as a volunteer learning to ride): get back in the saddle, even without stirrups, day after day, let your body be shaken until you no longer feel anything. Only if I kept digging and digging, would these muscle pains go away. Down at the well we had good news: breakfast was coming. Army coffee. And bread as well.

We had to march in a line back to where we had had dinner the night before. Again those huge kettles. Long benches had been placed in the yard. The Serbs were ladling out the coffee: alas, it was lukewarm by the time my turn came. Each man received half a kilo of bread, to last for two days. Our platoon commanders were slicing bacon for lunch, each portion the size of a matchbox, and rancid. The bread was coarse, but not inedible. (What was inedible these days?) During breakfast Dr Ferenc Bródy, our platoon's physician, joined me. He informed me in a whisper that the company physicians were conspiring to save me from physical labour; they would report that I had a severe organic heart condition. He would instruct me about the symptoms. Therefore I should report on sick call along with the seriously ill. And he begged my pardon for not thinking of this yesterday.

I said what you, dear reader, would have said in my place. As I was not sick, I could not take up the place of one of these severely ill, broken-down older men. I knew that very few were allowed to stay behind on sick call.

Nor did my vanity allow me to retreat. How despicable I would seem among all these slaves of the Pharaoh. I had as much right to suffer as any other man. Plus I did not regard digging the earthworks in such a tragic light.

This morning, too, the doctors were flooded with requests. The whining and wheedling sounded like so many beggars at a fair.

Already at reveille, back in the loft, a whole pack of

supplicants had descended on Dr Bródy and Dr Lukács, both of whom slept in my vicinity. They could hardly drive them off.

We were at the earthworks before six-thirty. I forgot to mention that on the previous evening we had to carry our tools to the storage shed in the back, and stack them neatly. Before that, we had to clean them. This was accomplished (and I know not who discovered the method) by two men facing each other, each scraping off the other's spade or shovel with his. In the morning before line-up we all went to get our tools; there was a crush for the shovels, as shovelling is easier than digging. There was much yelling and shoving and tussling to the accompaniment of that ugly, dumb clatter of tools.

Of course the second day was more miserable than the first. From six-thirty till noon we heard the scrape and slither of spade and shovel and the thud of the pickaxe. This morning there was another corporal waiting for us, a strapping lad with a handsome, swarthy, Kumanian face* – too bad his soul reflected none of the beauty. He was even louder than the onion-faced one; from the first, he looked at us as if we had murdered his father. All morning he leaped from one man to another, bashing the head or hitting the back of whoever was working at a slow pace, or tried to snatch a moment's breather. Onion-face, in turn, as if competing for some prize, gave out at least as many blows as the Kumanian. I found myself admiring the imposing artistry of the gentleman I had noted the day before for his ability as a shirker; even in the midst of these merciless slave-drivers he found a way to rest for five minutes after every five minutes of work, always managing to grab his shovel in the nick of time. (Of course he had secured a shovel today.) The swarthy corporal had one favourite refrain he used on everyone he attacked:

* A descendant of nomad Kumanians who settled in central Hungary during medieval times.

'Work too hard for you? Too hard? Easier to cheat people, huh?'

The other soldiers also kept busy, roughing up those miserable older men who were too slow in dragging and lifting their shovels.

A Tap on My Skull

I too had the honour of being hit. Across from me a thin little old man was straining to wield his shovel at a rapid pace.

I spoke to him in a fairly low voice:

'Take it easy, old man, you'll last longer.'

'Yapping? Yapping?' And I felt a blow on my head from behind. I had my hat on, and the blow slid off, so it didn't hurt, believe me. It was a slim, blond lad who hit me; I had already seen the day before how he loved to exercise his authority. The problem was not the blow, it was something else: it seemed so comical to be hit on the head at the age of sixty by a dumb boy that I was at pains not to laugh out loud. Imagine what would have happened if he had caught me laughing at him.

At noon our bacon was so rancid, stinking and salty that it was inedible. Most people spat out the first tentative bite (that is, those who tried it), and gave the meat away to those who wanted it. My bit of bacon became Steve's booty; again, he looked me up faithfully to inquire after my health. I saw him throw away a cigarette butt on the way; yet he still implored me with hands clasped: 'Man, I'm dying for a smoke!' He seemed to have forgotten that after breakfast he had already rolled a smoke from my tobacco tin.

This afternoon, too, we had to lay down several men for a rest.

On this second day we were dismissed at four-thirty, and this held for the following days.

For dinner, it was bean soup again, even more burnt than the day before. But never mind, we ate it.

Our Squad Leader

The morning brought a few small reforms. Those who stayed behind on sick call, if they could get about, were to clean up the loft and take the trash down. The two companies were separated; our company took my end of the loft, so I could keep my place. Near the back wall our company commander had a table, for he was expected to write out lists; at the side another table had been placed, on which the bread and bacon would be portioned out. Ambulatory invalids had to report at the forced labourers' kitchen in the back yard, to peel potatoes, shell peas and beans, carry firewood and water. Word had it from the office that this had been ordered by the Csomád command.

Before morning line-up our company commander divided each platoon into four squads of about sixteen men. I didn't see what difference this made in our platoon. Mr F. was appointed leader of our squad; he had received an awful fright when the engineer in charge of the platoon sprang this surprise on him. He was a thin, little, bespectacled man of about fifty-five, formerly bookkeeper at a silk store. As squad leader he was to keep order in the loft and at work, where he was to supervise us (though he was not exempt from work). Before marching out, Mr F. said in a plaintive voice:

'Gentlemen, if you please, this is a very touchy matter. I hate to yell at anyone, and don't know how to give orders; I have never given orders in my life.'

By the way, this morning I received coffee that was good and hot, into which I crumbled my bread like everyone else; it was more edible that way.

My sore muscles persisted; marching felt like lifting a pair of wooden legs. Others, too, complained of soreness. A delicate rain began to fall, so many soft pinpoints. Was this going to be a rainy day? But it turned out otherwise. In the morning and in the afternoon the rain kept starting to fall but stopped after a few minutes. Just like when you sit down to write a letter but get up after a few lines. The atmosphere remained hazy all day and was conducive to the saddest thoughts. There is not much to relate about the morning's work, laced as it was with the choicest curses, as before.

For lunch, again that mouthful of bacon. (We had brought our bread with us.) The same smelly, soft, rancid bacon. Since yesterday, I had been hearing the gentlemen wishing each other '*Mauvais appetit*'. I saved half of my bacon to grease my boots, the other half went to Steve, who always managed to find me. He confided that he was going on sick call; this earthworks was no job for a gentleman. Since he had taken off his trench coat you could see that his checked jacket had a large rip on the lapel. I asked him why he hadn't borrowed needle and thread to repair it. 'I hate to bother people,' he replied.

Shovel

Around three in the afternoon Dr L., my platoon commander, came over carrying a shovel. I was to hand over my spade and do some shovelling for a change; it was lighter work. True, digging was getting to be a nasty pain; I was panting like a dog. My back ached, and I was full of nervous tension, fed up with the monotony of this straining; from time to time the heat of passion would overwhelm me; it was all I could do not to fling away my spade and scream out.

So I went shovelling, about twenty paces back, in the second row. It was indeed much easier, the job of grading: spreading out the excavated soil and tamping it down with the back of the shovel.

A soldier yelled at one of my neighbours, who had stopped to wipe the sweat off his face with a handkerchief:

'Are you loafing, pops?'

When the man was not quick enough pocketing his handkerchief, up jumped our guard and smashed the man twice in the back so that his hat went flying in the dirt. He was a thin, lanky man with a wrinkled face, at least sixty years old. He picked up his faded hat and put it back on his head without daring to brush it off. He immediately started to shovel briskly. That faded Homburg must have bothered the soldier, for, eyeing it, he asked the man he had struck:

'What did you do as a civilian?'

The man answered in a hollow voice (he had throat cancer):

'Printer.'

The soldier paused for a moment as if in embarrassment, and then said:

'I'm sure you skimmed off the top.'

And he went away.

This expression had become popular in the last six or seven years. 'The Jews are always skimming' – taking the cream off the top. When this ideology began to spread, even delivery boys and market vendors were parroting its phrases. ('The Jews were always on the sunny side.') Whereas the Jews had more than their share of beggars.

The printer, or actually compositor, turned to me with a pathetic expression:

'What's this world coming to when they are hurting the innocent?'

Are You Innocent?

This job of grading was conducive to a bit of reflection. My thoughts picked on the printer, the innocent man. Most printers were organized into unions, and were socialists. And this innocent printer, and all the other loyal socialists, were the ones who had set and composed, that is blared out on the typesetting machine, all those editorials that led to war in 1914. Back then we had no radio. It was newspapers alone that had spread the contagion throughout society, the allure of playing war games, the exemption from the commandment 'Thou Shalt Not Kill'. Socialist printers typeset and broadcast all the lies and falsehoods, all those ungodly, incendiary incitements paid for by arms manufacturers. They did not seem to be shocked, they did not stop to look each other in the eye, but kept on working for the weekly wage. If only they had jumped up from the typesetting machines, and gone on strike, if only they had destroyed those printing presses! But no. And so the typesetting machines clattered away through those war years like so many machine guns, demanding war bonds and, like high priests, glorifying murder. I had always marvelled that printers would typeset anything that was said against their party, all those speeches in Parliament besmirching the names of revolutionaries, martyrs, exiles banished from the homeland.

The Slap

Well, the blow on the printer's back, and all the other blows administered by sticks on other backs, all that was nothing. Half an hour later we had to witness such a painful thing, such an atrocious act that (I am unable to complete this sentence). Our swarthy corporal screamed out – this was what made us look up –

'Why you dirty, lousy Jew!'

He was looking at the lawyer, Dr L., who stood facing him a few paces away, holding a pickaxe. Dr L. was a splendid-looking man, dressed in a hunting suit, knee stockings, hiking boots. He had a distinguished bearing. No trace of the 'birth defect' in his face. (Anyway, not two out of ten among us possessed 'obviously Jewish' looks.)

After yelling at Dr L., the corporal stepped up and gave him a tremendous slap in the face. Dr L. swayed but straightened out at once. A slight tremour flashed across his face, his shoulder jerked, and he seemed on the verge of moving forward. It appeared that, forgetting for a moment his family and everything else, he was going to throw himself on the corporal. The latter took a step back and kicked Dr L. in the stomach. His victim staggered backwards but amazingly did not fall – and it had been a tremendous kick. The corporal stepped up again and delivered another slap, and another and another, six or seven in all. For me, one of these would have been curtains. The corporal delivered the slaps with small pauses in between, as if he were gathering strength. Dr L. stood his ground like a rock, and the two men, throughout these slaps, continued to look into each other's eyes, hard.

Later, Dr L., whose face swelled up and turned dark red, said that he had been working at a steady pace and did not have the slightest idea what provoked the beating. It was his distinguished appearance; that, and his good clothes. The corporal lashed out at a Jew who dared to look like gentry.

Rag Rug

After half an hour I grew ashamed of the lighter work, and exchanged my shovel for a sweating man's spade.

There were roots twisting in the ground, some of them requiring a pickaxe. The spade had to be held vertically to chop at the root stems until they broke. Tiny pebbles and snails glinted and glittered in the soil, some of them looking like gold or silver. I, too, like many others, bent down quite often, believing I had found old coins or broken jewellery. The soil itself was even more fascinating, with its successive layers of yellow, purple, black, brown, bluish and greenish streaks. In some places the dig went as deep as two metres. I had a vision of the rag rug lying on the floorboards in my childhood. Its stripes had all these colours. What was in this soil, what made it so blue and green and lilac? I was ashamed that I did not know the chemistry of the soil, I did not know the soil that was our mother and our bread. At times my spade happened to slice earthworms in two, red ones and brown ones; I was sorry for them. Whenever I lifted my head for a breath of air, I would notice that clever gentleman who was able to snatch so many breathers; he was still doing what he did so well. Another squat little man, in a black leather jacket, was also sending furtive glances around, and whenever a guard or supervisor was not looking, would stop digging. He couldn't have been older than thirty. I wouldn't mind what he was doing, but we had an allotted amount of work every day, and these gentlemen looked on while the others, weaker, older, more infirm, did their work for them.

A Funeral

On the way back we saw another sad sight. At the edge of a sparse forest forced labourers were digging someone's grave in a ditch. They were already throwing the earth back on top of the grave. Two soldiers with armbands stood by the side. In the evening I heard they had been burying a 16-year-old boy who had diabetes. Those two soldiers had completely stripped the body, taken even his underwear, so he lay naked in the soil. The boy had been bunking in the other building, an only child, his father a dismissed civil servant. Who knows where he had been taken?

Blister

While on the march, people were comparing their blistered palms, some of them bleeding. What a pain it was to work with these blisters. I too had one on the palm of each hand, in spite of the gloves I wore. We needed Vaseline or Nivea cream, but where were we to get these? Many men had problems with their feet; inflamed corns or tight shoes hobbled quite a few. One gentleman who had lost his eyeglasses during lunch break was asking everyone if they had found them, a faraway, dreamy look in his eyes. Others complained of insomnia; even otherwise sound sleepers could not get any sleep here. (We also had our share of chronic insomniacs who had brought their sleeping pills, but ran out of these after a while. With each passing day these poor souls looked worse for wear.)

We marched to dinner under a cloudy sky that evening. Dinner was pea soup; as it was ladled out its burnt smell assaulted my nose. Still, an obnoxious pushing and shoving went on around the kettles. Undisciplined comrades jumped out of line to receive their food one minute earlier; from the sides and the rear arms would reach out with empty mess tins, people would squeeze ahead of others, shouting and cursing. The squad and platoon leaders reprimanded these in vain. There was also a type one might call criminal: those who, having wolfed down their portion, sneaked back in line for seconds. When caught, they would swear blind this was their first helping, and would fight furiously when they were elbowed out of the way. Because of such brigands, some evenings as many as a hundred had to go without food. We had all kinds among us: shoemakers, umbrella repairers, exterminators, janitors, porters, barkeepers, chauffeurs, news vendors, street hawkers, you name it.

One gentleman, who had lost his spoon, was eating his soup with a shoehorn.

Nor did Steve the sponger neglect me: like clockwork he turned up at dinnertime, offering to eat anything I did not like. He never failed to score a cigarette; alas, I had no more jam to offer. But I, too, enjoyed other folks' generosity: at lunchtime my neighbours from Pozsonyi Road treated me to canned goods, cheese, biscuits – I felt like a lord.

When we arrived back at the compound one of the forced labourers gave us the latest news from the noontime London broadcast (which they heard at the office). The Russians were advancing in the north; the night before they crossed seven passes in the Carpathians.

Thus each day we would receive a brief summary of news from London.

Albert Havas looked me up every day to inquire if I needed anything. One day he brought me six delicious little apples. He would not accept any money. 'When we are back home in Budapest.'

He even offered me some money, for the forced labourers under Captain Megay's command were allowed to keep theirs.

Rainy Day

The next day it rained. The drizzle at dawn helped us wash ourselves, and cooled our coffee.

We began digging in the rain. The earthworks were intended to be tank traps; the idea was that the Russian tanks and armoured cars would bog down in this three-metre-deep ditch.

I forgot to mention that one anonymous gentleman dubbed our stint at Erdőváros a 'jamboree'.

The rain did not pelt us, it merely soaked us with a steady, thin stream. There were no umbrellas; and anyway, you would have had to have a third arm to hold one while digging or shovelling. Only three soldiers kept guard over us that day, wandering around, looking bored, letting out an occasional bark like watchdogs who want to make sure they don't forget the knack.

A man's biography consists of his thoughts. Everything else that happens to me is something alien. As we slipped and slid around in that mud the work was slowed down, providing an occasion for more conscious reflection. We are always thinking about something, although we may not pay attention to our thoughts. Now, writing ten months after the events, I cannot recall a speck of what I had been thinking then. But I do remember trying to recall the thoughts of that day on the march back. And I was unable to recover a single snippet of what my mind had dug up during that day. Thoughts sink into forgetfulness as quickly as rain into the earth.

More Slaps

It was that swarthy corporal again. He had to show off on this day as well. It hurts all over to recall this. As we were marching through Erdőváros, we saw our dark corporal standing there talking to a civilian. We tried to march by

quietly, in strict order (small wonder, in view of the execu-
tioner). The so-called company ahead of us had already
marched past when the corporal yelled for Mr K., the engineer in charge of that company. Mr K. stopped in front of the
corporal, his wet yellow leather coat glistening. We could not
hear what was said, if anything, but ten seconds later we
saw the corporal raise his arm and strike the engineer with
the same violence he had used the day before on Dr L.
Imagine, if you can, the impact of this slap on the mind and
body of Mr K. But he held his ground and did not move. And
just like on the day before, the corporal struck his victim's
face full force seven or eight times, at measured intervals.
Our company had halted; I was staring at the mud by my
feet, and heard nothing but those resounding slaps.

That swarthy fellow had to extract vengeance for his
own subordinate position on yet another good-looking and
well-dressed gentleman.

We marched back to the compound in silence.

Mr K. immediately went up to the loft and did not come
down for dinner.

Before dinner, having brought down our eating uten-
sils and washed our hands at the well, we all walked or stood
around in the yard; sitting down, God forbid, would have
meant not being able to get up again.

This evening, Mr F., our squad leader, tendered his res-
ignation from the dignity of his post. On this day, with the light
guard, many gentlemen had slacked off. Mr F. felt hurt by this
lack of solidarity, but it was not his nature to scold and yell,
therefore he asked to be relieved from his command.

This One, That One

We had one especially wretched person in our midst, with the most severe depression. He was a short, chubby young man of about thirty, with a priestly face. No one knew who he was. He just stood, looking down at the ground, until people would lay him down to rest. When talked to, he did not talk back. When he was taken out to work on the first day, and given a shovel, he stood there motionless. The doctor quickly led him away by the arm, so he would not be harmed. Since then he had stayed back with the seriously ill. But he would not even peel potatoes. All day long he sat up in the loft and stared at the straw. He had to be brought down for breakfast and dinner, and hand-fed coffee and soup.

Another one: a poorly dressed, thin, pale man, also youngish. He never talked to anyone. While we were waiting for dinner, or as we milled about in the morning before breakfast, he would walk up and down at a distance, as far as he could get away to be all by himself. With his hands clasped together like a child he walked looking up, up at the sky. Otherwise he came to work and wielded the shovel.

A third one wept all the time. He was around forty or forty-two, sickly, and wore the clothes of the petty bourgeoisie. He kept crying, crying all the time. The doctors thought he was a neurotic. He was mourning his aged parents and all his siblings, who had been taken away to Germany. His tears were always falling, even while on the march; he kept dabbing at his eyes with a handkerchief that was never out of his hand. At times, around lunch break, or when we clambered up into the loft at bedtime, he sobbed out loud. He received much sympathy (others had wept by his side), and many tried to console him with words or a caress. But his weeping was unstoppable.

On that first afternoon here, when we were still idling around, a gentleman about my age introduced himself: Mr N. N., forced into retirement from an office job. Five minutes later, when I was alone, he strolled back to me.

'Maestro, do you happen to recall that chapter from Herodotus where he says . . .' (and here followed a slew of ancient Greek).

'I am sorry, I don't know any Greek, I dropped out.'

'He wrote that about the Peloponnesian War.'

He went into an explanation of similarities between the ancient Peloponnesian and current Hungarian situations, but my mind wasn't really there. The next morning he collared me by the well:

'Aurora juvis amica.'

During the line-up after work he managed to be at my side; whether by accident or plan I know not.

'Perhaps you recall these four lines of Schiller's: "Da werden Weiber zu Hyänen/ Und treiben mit Entzetzen Scherz,/ Noch zuckend mit des Panters Zähnen,/ Zerreisen sie des Feindes Herz." A propos this, I want to tell you . . .'

The next morning he quoted Cicero, the day after a strophe of Camoens, in Portuguese.

I asked him if he spoke Portuguese.

'Oh, it is a beautiful tongue; I recommend it heartily, Maestro. You should learn Portuguese.'

The Roof

I must report the roof of the drying loft: it had numerous leaks. Around ten at night (for us, the middle of the night), when, in spite of the noisy squabbles and snores, I had managed to fall asleep, I was roused by raindrops falling on my head. It was raining, and it rained all night. I don't know how many of us managed to get any sleep. I covered my face with my towel, but it was soon soaked. I would snatch three or four minutes of sleep at a time before waking shivering. This was how my neighbours spent the night too.

Mud

My eyes were aflame, and so were my nerves, at dawn when we had to get up in pitch-darkness.

Half an hour later the rain at last stopped. But we still held to the hope that we would not have to go to work this day, for the ground was soaked. Any minute the order for us to stay at quarters should be arriving. But no such order came. We were still expecting that order as we marched out through the gate.

Yes, we had to work on, slipping and sliding through the mud, getting stuck in puddles. Several of us fell down. The spade was impossible to lift, with so much mud sticking to it. Soft as the ground was, our guards managed to be as hard; never before had we received so many curses and blows. Corporal Onion-face (absent the day before) was there to make up for it by extra helpings of meanness.

For lunch we were given jam instead of bacon. It was sweet, but only a mouthful. This stint at Erdőváros would be a boon to the stouter gentlemen, who could now skip taking the Karlsbad cure this year.

In the afternoon Onion-face drove a line of shovellers down into the deepest part of the ditch. It was less than one metre wide at the bottom. The corporal shoved me forward to join them with my spade.

'Move it! Move it!'

With great difficulty I slid down to the bottom of the ditch, into the mud and puddles, with my low shoes. I was supposed to toss the earth that fell into the ditch back up, three metres high.

Let me pass in silence over the torments of this operation. Onion-face kept coming back to check on us; he howled at us and once or twice grabbed at his holster. That muddy soil kept falling back off the sides of the ditch; no one among us had the strength to heave it as high as three metres. Ankle-deep in cold water, straining without any results, I reached a point where I thought I would go stark raving mad. It was amazing I did not collapse. That night I was unable to sleep a wink. Poor, fragile Dr Bálint next to me was also unable to sleep. Many others were sleepless that night.

I got up with a cold the next morning. At least another hundred of my companions were sneezing and coughing.

Korányi and Pásztor

As if in compensation for the day before, fate served up a pleasant surprise in the morning. Our coffee was being served by Zoltán Korányi, of the Café Royal, for he, too, was one of us. And reigning over the neighbouring cauldron was Zoltán Pásztor, Korányi's brother-in-law, who had been an actor in his youth. Korányi was limping and Pásztor had a heart condition. They ended up on the sick-list, doing kitchen work; dinner would be cooked by Korányi from now on. He had had a little restaurant in Paris for a few years until the arrival of the German visitors made him come home.

In the evening he made us a bean soup that left us licking all ten fingers.

Butts

If you are not familiar with butts, hold up your hand. This designation for cigarette stubs has always appealed to me for some reason.

I have not mentioned it so far, but the poorer sort among us had begun to ask for butts as early as the third day.

By the sixth day I alone had four clients who waited for me regularly at mealtimes, to receive my cigarette butts. Their anticipation made me so anxious that I could not smoke my cigarettes all the way down, and handed them over with a good third remaining. I had also discovered a technique for making the cigarette last longer. After each inhale I would stop up the opening of the cigarette holder to allow less smoke to escape and make the tobacco burn slower. I told everyone about this invention and did not apply for a patent. I began to notice dreamily loitering comrades, and not only the poorest ones, here and there in the compound, bending down to pick up a butt. Some of them did look around furtively to see if anyone was looking.

A Small Accident

I had a small accident on the sixth day of work. Because the ditches were beginning to fill up with water, a pump had been carted over from Csomád that morning. Six older men were assigned to operate the pump on planks laid across the ditch.

Around two in the afternoon engineer L. asked me politely if I cared to help with the pump for a while. This was considered an easier task than digging. As I was ready to collapse any minute, I accepted. The engineer made sure to switch the men on this job every hour, but he left me there all afternoon. The pump handle had to be moved up and down, and five minutes of this was enough to make one's arm and shoulder ache, especially if you were as exhausted as we were, without sleep and weakened by a cold. To do this all day was punishment fit for an inferno.

Well, around four-thirty we had to roll up the lines and pull the pump on its cart over to the side. I grabbed the cart shaft near the base, and as we turned, a terrific pain stabbed my right hand. My index and middle fingers had got caught in a wheel. The cart was stopped and rolled back; when my hand was freed blood was pouring from the two fingernails. After washing the wounds and applying iodine the doctor bandaged my hand. I thought some bones in my fingers were broken, my hand was so badly mangled by that evil wheel.

Doing Nothing

Naturally I could no longer work with a spade or shovel. I wasn't much use around the kitchen either, for I couldn't touch anything with my wounded hand.

I found my enforced idleness bitter. I was not writing and had nothing to read. Around noon one of the forced labourers gave me a detective novel to read, but I could not make it past page three. I could never read more than one or two stories by Conan Doyle, nor did I go for Nick Carter in my schoolboy days, any more than for algebra.

I sat on the bench next to the invalids who were peeling potatoes, shelling peas and beans, washing dishes. I loitered and watched the forced labourers work, and walked around the compound looking at the fine landscape. (Word had it that people from Budapest were beginning to buy lots in the neighbourhood.) Behind the workers' quarters I saw a patch of unusual spotted and striped melons, and was told these were winter melons, which kept their savour and freshness all season.

I stopped in at the tailor's shop where two forced labourers were working. One of them had had a shop in Paris, the other was a milliner from Budapest. As a favour they kindly ironed my trousers. There were two workers in the shoe-repair shop: one a former shoe manufacturer, the other a shoe wholesaler. All relatives of both men had been carried off to Germany. Another young forced labourer, who happened to stop in at the shop, favoured me with a shave. He had been a dental technician.

Thus my first day of sick call dragged by. The sun has to set every day.

Bricks

The next day Herr Direktor T. joined me in sick bay. I had known him at the Fészek Club, where he used to play bridge. He was a patron of the arts. As the air up in the loft was very stale, he got up in the afternoon to hobble about on his injured foot. We had to keep an eye out for Arrow Cross men coming through the gate.

As Mr T.'s business interests in the past had included a brick factory, he was able to fill me in about bricks. He told me that this was the largest brick factory in the country. The bricks manufactured here were the modern-type clinkers (also known as 'hard' or 'vitrified' bricks). These large, heavy, sturdy clinkers were used as facing bricks, mostly in state-sponsored constructions such as schools or hospitals. Clinkers were five times more expensive than ordinary wall-bricks; before the war they ran as high as 200 pengős per thousand. (Bricks are sold by the thousand.) Furthermore, Mr T. enlightened me that the reddish colour of bricks was not due to paint, but was a result of the baking process. This is what I learned about bricks at Erdő'város.

This and That

The next day I was looking for my remaining tobacco in my bag but couldn't find it. It was gone. And it seemed to me that a shirt and one or two handkerchiefs were also missing from that overstuffed bag.

For days I had been hearing complaints about thefts.

Our company commander announced that anyone caught stealing would be handed over to the Arrow Cross men.

According to the latest news the Russians had reached Gödöllő.

There followed a debate about the fate of Hungary. Of course, the outcast Jews evinced a desperate patriot's concern about their country's future. The consensus was that anyone hoping for a German victory had to be a traitor. If the Germans were to win the war, there would be nothing left of Hungary.

We were amazed with each passing day that the present regime was able to hold out. Back in Budapest we had thought the Szálasi takeover would last a week to ten days.

One of the forced labourers, who had just returned from an errand in Budapest, told us that Jewish women between the ages of 16 and 42 were being taken away on work details.

Dr Bálint joined me among the invalids. It was his heart. He helped out in the kitchen. As for his heart, he had been told that, without undue excitement, it would last another thirty years. (Later that winter this fine man, too, was killed.)

Our company commander announced that we were allowed to write home one postcard each week. He passed out the cards and reminded us about the censorship. Later, back in Budapest, we found out that none of the cards had been forwarded.

The forced labourers' kitchen was run by a Mr B., who was a good cook. They had meat with their noontime meal each day. He gave me and Dr Bálint a plate of vegetables for lunch, which we ate hiding out in a room. On some days Mr B. was able to put aside a small portion of meat for us. He was an educated man, 36 years old, and showed us photos of his wife and two beautiful children who were hiding out with false papers. When he wasn't cooking, Mr B. walked up and down in the yard, alone and head to the ground, no doubt thinking about his family.

This morning a well-dressed gentleman among the invalids approached one of the forced labourers, who was eating a piece of bacon, and inquired: 'May I have first option on the bacon skin?'

I saw another gentleman picking up a crust of bread from the mud.

Our four doctors were besieged by the ailing. One man with haemorrhoids was unable to take another step without his Anusol; others were begging for pain killers, sedatives, pills and tablets, none of which was available.

One gentleman broke his glasses; another had lost them. This latter was stumbling around like a sleepwalker, feeling his way about with outstretched arms.

Even Dr Bródy came to resemble his patients, sick with worry for his one and only daughter, a beauty (judging by her photo) – afraid she would be taken away. She had graduated with an outstanding record from high school, spoke four languages, wanted to be a chemist, but had to work as an optician's assistant. She was also a teacher of eurhythmics.

Our company had four fine physicians: Professor Dénes Fuchs and Drs Ferenc Bródy, Jenő Garai and Pál Lukács. The last named was a dear friend from my student days.

In the other company a seriously ill person had died on each of the last two days.

A Bombing

Every day we heard air-raid sirens from far off. On our eighth night here we had a close call, and a very ugly one at that.

Around midnight we were woken by terrific explosions. The whole loft was lit up like broad daylight. Again and again we were shaken by enormous explosions caused by the giant bombs called *Bezirksbombe* in German. Over the explosions and the sound of airplane engines we could hear alarm sirens from three directions.

We thought they must have targeted the brick factory, taking it for some kind of munitions plant. We had no shelter. We were not permitted to run down to the yard. And what good would it have done, anyway.

It was like high noon up in the loft. And those bombs felt as if they were exploding next door.

The weaker among us were wailing. Across from me, a man muttered prayers as he sat up with his hands clasped. Of course almost everyone sat or stood up, as if that lessened the danger. This brought a cacophony of shouts, as hands and feet were stepped upon. I just sat there, my heart pounding. I did not fear death but I dreaded the loss of an arm or a leg. The thought flashed through my mind that it would be fitting to die now, and not survive the devastation of my country.

I saw, not for the first time, that one did not fear death in its immediate presence. Thinking stops at such times. Within seconds a process of shutting off takes over within the brain, so that the mind (and, we might say, the soul) rejects, refuses to acknowledge all the horrors accosting us. There is a beautiful wisdom in this built-in self-defence.

This crisis must have lasted an hour and a quarter.

After it I may or may not have slept; lest we forget, the bedding was hard brick and the nights were getting colder. Left and right I heard sighs until the break of dawn.

The next day we learned that the Russians had bombed a nearby German armoured vehicle and truck depot.

One gentleman said: 'I am an atheist, but last night I prayed.'

Swedish and Swiss Hopes

On the ninth day of our 'jamboree' the news came that the Szálasi regime, obeying international pressure, had restored the validity of passes issued by foreign governments.

Great was the rejoicing among the Israelites – among the Israelites protected by the Swedish, Swiss and Portuguese passes – and even among those who had been granted exemptions by Governor Horthy. (These latter were also revalidated by the regime, in an effort to make its action more plausible.)

The 'Swedes' and the 'Swiss' all thought that they could tear off their yellow stars and start heading home immediately.

Those over sixty again started to complain about being held here illegally; when would something be done about them? Several days ago we had received word from the office that those over sixty would be allowed to go. But nothing had come of it, so far.

It was remarkable to see how many had Swiss or Swedish or Governor's passes. At night, before lights out, they all lined up in front of engineer Marton's desk, to have their names listed. Each night the candle burned late on this table, where the company and platoon commanders made up their lists of those on sick call, and did paperwork. Another table at the far exit was used for the same purpose.

I had not brought my pass with me; luckily I had a paper in my wallet with the number of my Swedish pass on it.

So our names would be forwarded to Csomád the next morning. We hoped we would be able to leave the following afternoon.

But day after day went by and nothing happened.

What Happened to Our Rights?

I admired His Excellency G., a retired judge. He had no Swedish pass, but was over sixty, and was expecting to be released on this count. After all, they should never have brought him, along with others his age.

'What happened to our rights?' he shouted again today. 'I ask you: What happened to our rights?'

Ever since we had been brought here, I had been hearing this refrain from His Excellency: What happened to our rights?

I tried to imagine how many thousands of times, over the past thirty years, he had had to ponder this question: What happened to our rights, our inalienable human rights? He refused to accept that there were no human rights these days, that they had been relegated, like ancient armour, to museums.

Seven Girls

One of the army guards was telling us in the kitchen that last night a company of Jewish women and girls had been brought to Csomád, and they were already out digging and shovelling early this morning. He was amazed to see how cheerfully they marched through Csomád, singing all the way. He saw many good-looking ones among them (and here he expressed in a few plain words his desire to court these beauties).

At night we heard that seven girls had tried to escape from Csomád after lunchtime. Three of them had been shot by the Arrow Cross henchmen, and four were captured.

Dr Bródy was feverish with anxiety, and so were many others here whose wives and daughters must have been taken, perhaps to Csomád, who knows. And what if . . .

Monday, Tuesday, Wednesday

Every day was the same, the only difference being what we had for dinner: beans or potatoes. One evening someone brought the news that on the morrow a Red Cross truck would be here to take those with Swedish passes. The following day this proved to be pure fantasy.

Or else the difference between yesterday and today was that one morning the well ran dry and we were allowed only a handful of water to wash in.

My injured fingers were swollen and purple, and the

slightest pressure on the bandage hurt unbearably. The doctors said it would take a long time to heal.

People were talking about poor Endre Frank in front of the kitchen. He had been such a sweet and charming man. One of the gentlemen voiced his opinion:

'When this is over, all the best and most righteous Jews will have died, and only the dross will remain.'

At last I had a chance to take a bath. (I had postponed it because of my cold.) I had a bucket of warm water to stand in and soaped myself down from top to toe. Then I washed my shirt, socks, handkerchief.

I forgot to mention that a week ago we were required to hand over any shirts in excess of two per person.

For the first two or three days those who had blades would shave religiously during their early morning toilette. Others, who had been used to going to the barber for their shave, remained unshaven. By the fourth or fifth day the shavers began to be less zealous; most of them got up too exhausted and depressed to shave, and hurried to fall into line. By the tenth day even the best-dressed and most dignified gentlemen sported beards that would have done honour to bandits or murderers. This morning we had to separate two gentlemen who got into fisticuffs over who had whose shovel. How did he know which shovel was his? Well, he had marked his initials on the handle; go take a look.

I was in constant torment about this enforced inactivity, about the loss of all this precious time, never to be replaced.

My 'kinsman', Péter Pál Szép, had brought me some tobacco leaf. Who would cut it for me? We found a Romanian prisoner who undertook the job for a quarter share, and chopped me some fine cigarette tobacco.

Lest I forget: the sponging artist also joined us in sick bay. He claimed an arthritic condition, if my memory serves.

He did nothing all day except squabble. But he always managed to have a smoke.

I had the additional honour of meeting a corporal of the guard, who introduced himself to me in front of the kitchen. A tall, blond young man, he had just returned from leave. He at once invited me, the 'Maestro', for lunch in his small room near the kitchen. Pork chops. Apples. Red wine (ugh, a sour red wine). The corporal was a locksmith, who preferred to read when the others played cards. He played his accordion in my honour. A few days later he surprised me with three little packages of pipe tobacco, which enabled me to make three pipe smokers very happy. They had been down to smoking dry leaves, just like some of the desperate cigarette smokers. Cigar smokers suffered the most; neither pipe nor cigarettes satisfied their craving.

One comrade had a sad complaint: two days before we were rounded up in Budapest, he had 13 teeth pulled; he had been scheduled to receive his dentures just about now. The only way he could eat bread was by soaking it in coffee. 'Try to imagine my difficulty until we were given our first soup.' He used to be a stockroom manager at a vinegar factory.

Hitler

In the afternoon, when the amateur pick-and-shovel men returned from work, the interested parties, those with Swiss, Swedish and other passes, got together to discuss why nothing had been done about them. While everyone stood around, and milled about until dinnertime, groups of all sizes formed and the air buzzed with talk.

I joined my neighbours from Pozsonyi Road, who were hashing over Hitler.

Someone mentioned that Hitler had not given a speech in a long time.

Another one chimed in: 'Is the monster still alive?'

This had been a lively topic ever since the attempt on Hitler's life that summer. Opinions varied: he was alive, but dared not address the populace, or else he'd been stripped of power and was a mere figurehead; or he was no longer alive, the bomb tore him apart in June, and ever since then he had been impersonated by a look-alike.

A third gentleman added: 'Who cares if he's alive or not; the main thing is that the Teutons be crushed.'

A fourth: 'I would rather he lived, so the beast could be punished.'

A fifth: 'And how would you punish him? Can there be sufficient punishment for a man like that? Are there enough hells?'

And a sixth: 'I think he should be hanged once for each life he's destroyed. That's an old Chinese law. The murderer was hanged once for each victim. He was cut down at the last moment and taken back to prison. He would never know when he would be taken again, for the final time.'

The fourth one came back with: 'My good man, who can tell how many millions of times you'd have to hang Hitler.'

A hoarse voice took over:

'Gentlemen, this is what I would do with him: put him in a cage in the London zoo. In a special place of honour, where people would pay separate admission. And every visitor could spit in his eye. He would be force-fed so he'd stay alive. And all the money collected would go to indigent Jews and to the poor of every other nation destroyed by that scoundrel.'

(I must say the cage was not this man's invention, we'd been hearing about it for years.)

Someone else came up with an improvement:

'He should not be confined to the London zoo, but taken all over the continent, and to America, Australia, all over. Just like Barnum's circus used to exhibit the hunger artist and the dog-headed Russian, back in my childhood. I saw the Barnum circus in Makó.'

After this, the orchestra director J. spoke up. He was a greying, lanky man, always with a wan, sad smile on his Don Quixote face. He had been dismissed from an opera company in Germany.

'If you will allow me, gentlemen, I will tell you the punishment I have imagined for him whose name will not pass my lips. This is in case he survives, and does not commit suicide before being captured. I have a feeling, gentlemen, this would be the only punishment that could possibly fit the crimes of this horrible figure.'

'Well, what would it be? Let's hear it! Silence, everybody!'

'That he should live forever, and never die, never.'

Someone laughed.

'Whew!'

'That's right, my dear friends, he should live forever. Unable to die by bullet, drowning, poison, suicide. No one should lay a finger on him. Let a thousand years go by, a hundred thousand; let the sun grow cold, and not a blade of grass, not a single creature remain alive save him. In darkness, in silence, let him be the only being left alive. God may die, but this man should stay alive for ever, and never go mad, always keep remembering.'

There was silence for half a minute. I could hear someone mutter near me: 'That's horrible.'

The orchestra director gave a small laugh. 'That's right. I thought it up the night my 79-year-old mother was taken away in a cattle wagon.'

Again there was silence. Another man, whose face was familiar from the streets of Budapest, added: 'Remember what we used to say about him a year or two ago? Here was the man who had succeeded in making the whole world miserable.'

I could hear the sighs going up (mine included).

Another man laughed: 'And what a ridiculous face! The ruler of a huge empire, and I had to laugh seeing his face in the papers day after day! And not even that little moustache is original, he stole that from Chaplin.'

'Do you know what he really looks like?' asked Mr M., a lawyer. 'He looks like those underworld characters who are featured in pornographic photographs.'

'That's right! Absolutely! You said it!' There was laughter all around.

But an elderly gentleman reverted to a serious note.

'And still, let's face it, the man is a genius.'

Hitler, that is.

There was this unbelievable readiness among the Jews, even before the war, to credit Hitler with being a genius. Hitler, and even Goebbels. I can still hear the hundreds of male and female voices echoing: 'You've got to hand it to them! That Hitler is a genius! Goebbels is a genius!' They were convinced that this was a sign of intelligence, to admit, in public, that Hitler or Goebbels was a genius. To acclaim as genius the very men who would cover you with filth and torment you to death! In a hypnotic trance they parroted: 'Hitler is a genius!'

Another comrade said:

'Hitler must be insane, without a doubt.'

'That's right, he cannot be normal.'

'I tell you, they should have admitted him to art school,

then we would not have any of these problems.'

'It's interesting that Hitler's name begins with an *H*, same as Haman.'*

'And hyena!'

Next I heard the voice of a former university professor:

'There is no need to delve into personalities here, into names; no need to look for individuality. I do not regard him as a human being, as one of us. I consider him to be a Golem; look at the way he walks and moves, you've seen it in the newsreels. Even his physiognomy, look at it, there is nothing human about it; he is made of mud; he is a machine, a puppet; or else think of him as a snowman, stuck together and stood up on its feet. The ones responsible for this snowman are Treitschke, Hegel, List, Gobineaux, all the way back to Frederick the Great – how many other names do we need? But instead of snow, they used some kind of German germ as their material. German presumption, the stupidity of millions, their superstitions and cruelties.'

We all stayed quiet for a while. But one refined soul said with a smirk: 'Who was that idiot?'

Thou Shalt Not Steal

God's commandment was not necessarily obeyed here where there was no police and no court to enforce it.

Even during the forced labour in Egypt the Jews must have been stealing from each other, and that was why Moses brought down the Seventh Commandment from Mount Sinai.

---

* The Jewish festival of Purim celebrates the delivery of the Jews from the massacre plotted by their enemy Haman in the time of Artaxerxes.

Yesterday someone stole my soap, today, my towel.

I managed to obtain a small piece of soap from a forced labourer. As for a towel, I saw one drying in the kitchen and offered to buy it. The owner, a 16-year-old boy who worked in the kitchen, would not accept the money I could have easily borrowed from a friend. He took his one and only towel, cut it in half, and gave me one piece.

Every day there were more and more complaints about food, razors, combs, soap, toothpaste, handkerchiefs, socks, cigarettes disappearing from knapsacks. Our company commanders threatened a general search of all bags. But this was never carried out; it would have been too humiliating.

An old barber told with tears in his eyes about a hand reaching under his pillow before dawn. That was where he had hidden a fine piece of bacon he had bartered from a soldier in exchange for his belt. This morning he had thought he was dreaming, but the bacon was gone when he woke up. At noon he saw the gentleman who was his left-hand neighbour making a meal of this bacon.

'It was my bacon, I could tell by the red-brown paper it was wrapped in.'

'Well, and why didn't you run over and knock it out of his hand, and slap him in the face?'

'God forbid, he is a very wealthy man, he owns several buildings.'

People laughed right into his tear-soaked face.

'How can you be such an idiot?'

No, he was not an idiot, just a poor man who respected the wealthy.

Not Very Amusing

We made a sickroom out of a small tool shed, to be used by the women working at Csomád. This morning two patients were brought in, a young woman and a girl. The two of them shared a single bed made of boards. The young woman had had a miscarriage; the girl had TB, and was vomiting blood. I looked in on them. The woman lay there as pale as plaster of Paris, her eyes closed. We had no pain-killers to relieve her.

The worst ugliness of Hitlerism was this utter lack of chivalry. Women were its victims just the same. It forced the manicure girl out of her job, and put a shovel in the hands of a woman in her sixth month of pregnancy. I expected Hitler's crew to drop down on all fours at any moment, instead of walking on two feet like true human beings.

There was nothing here to allay the gall bladder attacks, bleeding ulcers, floating kidneys, hernias, not to speak of the many lesser complaints: diarrhoea, constipation, bladder infections, influenza, inflamed eyes, arthritic pains.

And buttons popped, and shoes wore out, their owners hobbling about. Jackets and trousers were getting looser as everyone was losing weight. One comrade stopped every passer-by with: 'Do you have a safety pin?'

Is there anyone who still remembers the clown with the green nose in the Beketow Circus of long ago? He kept grabbing at his pantaloons that were always slipping off, as he shuffled by the first row, asking everyone: 'Have you got a pin? Have you got a pin?'

Another tell-tale bit of misery I saw: a crumpled ball of newsprint in someone's aching ear, in place of a cotton ball.

When Are We Going to Leave?

Only the good Lord knows. Every night they made a list of the Swedish and Swiss passes, and the Governor's exemptions, and each morning we awaited our release.

Herr Direktor T., in a gesture of self-sacrifice, even limped over to the Csomád command post (accompanied by an armed guard) to expedite matters.

The others kept congratulating those about to be liberated, but this was beginning to sound like mockery. And one had to feel ashamed in front of these considerate comrades who had no Swedish or Swiss or other kinds of exemptions and who would have to stay on and suffer here.

And there was the added danger that our Arrow Cross guards would massacre the whole lot of us when the Russians arrived, or else herd us off towards the west.

A Nasty Day

On the night of the eleventh or twelfth day a heavy rain began to fall. We were soaked while eating our dinner, and after we had taken shelter in the loft it kept raining all night long. I have already entertained you with an account of what a rainy night was like.

And the next morning it was still pouring, as if this were some island in Oceania where the coming of winter was signalled by six weeks of rain.

Again, the men expected to stay back at quarters, for the earthworks were impossible on a day like this.

But they had to march out.

They got back at ten at night. Out by the earthworks they had been met by a single guard, and he too had left, with the order that they were to stay until half past four. Of course it was impossible to get any work done in the mud and puddles. You may imagine the lot of those wretches that day. No chance to sit or walk, just stand around in the downpour. Many were unable to control themselves and wept.

They started back in the dark, and got lost. Some slipped into ditches and pits, and emerged with twisted ankles.

It is impossible to describe the way the company looked the next day. These poor men were desperate. Dozens reported sick.

Why were they doing this to us? Every day we were newly amazed at the way propaganda had embedded itself into the young minds of our guards. And by now it was obvious that this whole earthworks project had been invented solely for our torment.

A Crust of Bread and Such

Mr R. had a tale about one peculiar customer. He himself would always cut off the crust of his bread, because of all the hands that touched it, and had found a 'client' for his bread-crusts, a poor man who had been a pedlar of coat-hangers. This man joined him regularly at mealtimes, ten days running, to pick up his bread-crusts.

'Yesterday morning,' said Mr R., 'I was so darned hungry that I ate even the crust. Well, when my client came, I had nothing for him. He stalked off in anger. At noon I controlled myself and left him his crust. But he would not come for it. Before we went back to work, I took it over to him. But he would not accept it. He yelled at me that I should eat it myself! And I couldn't pacify him at night, either. He turned away when I went over to him. And today I hear he's been telling everyone that I am a filthy swine, a thief even. What can you do with such a miserable wretch? I can understand he wants to punish me, but why does he punish himself? Wouldn't it be better for him to chew on my bread-crust?'

Steve the artist had been caught in the kitchen stuffing himself with sweetened coffee cubes that were meant for all of us. And he had had the gall to raise his voice, shouting that the doctors recommended this as a cure for his nerves!

As for me, I even had a little dream last night about eating beef. I had other similar little dreams: drinking cognac, or sitting at Prunier's in Paris, where they placed in front of me my regular *demi* of Saint Emilion. I sipped the wine slowly, for in my dream I was aware of being at Erdőváros, where this good red wine was a rare blessing indeed.

In the middle of the night I woke with a start: I felt a bite! Did I have lice? But no, it was only a bit of straw under my shirt.

The Jewish Question

One of the comrades on sick call had a chat with an army guard. This is the account he gave:

'How stupid can you get, I ask you, what are the limits of human stupidity! This soldier was telling me that it was an ugly thing the Jews were doing in Budapest; he's heard they go up on rooftops at night to signal to the bombers where to drop their bombs. So I tell him: listen, friend, do you think the Jews are that dumb, to call for bombs on the building they live in? And what do you think, what kind of signals could they send? Anyone caught with a lamp or lighting a candle would be shot on the spot. And how else could they signal? Think about it, the airplanes are at an altitude of 5,000 metres; would they see someone waving at them in the dark? How could he swallow such inanities? So he tells me he heard it from someone who came from Budapest and the man doesn't lie.'

Years ago I heard an old friend tell about sitting in a café at a retired general's table, where several other high-ranking officials were congregated. 'One of the generals complained indignantly about that renegade Petschauer, who switched over to the Bolshevik side, and now he was guiding the Bolshie bombers to the public buildings to be destroyed, for he was the only one who knew Budapest like that! Imagine the stupidity! I remonstrated in vain, asking them how they could believe such fairy tales; they shouted me down. When it comes to the topic of Jews, their intelligence goes out like a light. I had to blush for them.'

Once, about three years ago, I went to the Jewish Museum to look at an exhibition of pictures. I saw two children pecking in at the museum door. The girl must have been around thirteen and the boy about seven.

'Would you like to come in?'

'We are not allowed, we are Christians.'

'That's all right, come on in,' and I extended my hand towards the little girl.

'Oh no, because the Jews will kill us,' and she grabbed the little boy's hand.

'Do you go to school?' I asked. They were both barefoot.

'Oh yes. I'm in the fourth grade.' And they ran off.

So this was the result of the good teachers' work.

And ever since Stalingrad the extreme right wing of the press had been busy spreading the word that if Germany were to lose the war, *the Jews would exterminate the Christians.* And this was swallowed by adults, by people with degrees; the so-called middle class passed this depraved nonsense from mouth to mouth. As my old friend said, it short-circuited their brains. They were able to believe that the Jews would exterminate their own clients. And whom would they cheat, whom would they live off, after that? And how could they believe, the sons of this brave Hungarian nation, that a handful of Jews would exterminate ten million Gentiles? Even counting the Jewish babes in arms, there were no more than 150,000 of us left; weak, unarmed Jews. Couldn't the Gentiles conceive of resisting such an onslaught? After all, they would not have to kneel down and offer their necks to be cut . . .

Oh, this was the greatest suffering, the one meted out on one's intelligence. To have to swallow this thick spate of idiocy, to breathe this filthy smog instead of clean air; all these lies, all these stupefying inanities. To look on helplessly at the mental degradation of this country blessed with such human resources and talent, to witness this atrophy of reason, spirit, humour. When would we ever recover from the damage done to the mind and soul of this nation? There was one explanation for otherwise intelligent people believing these wild inanities about the Jews. When you usurp another people's jobs, businesses and properties, it is easy to believe all the bad things about them, to justify the hatred, and lull the conscience.

On this day I had heard a number of Jewish debates, as we milled around before dinner.

'But I am still a nationalist,' said one man, about forty-five years of age.

An older man reacted to this: 'But what if your nation does not accept you as a Hungarian?'

'That's only today's mentality; I refuse to acknowledge it.'

The other man merely waved his hand and turned away, smiling.

'What I want to know,' someone asked, 'is why do they hate us?'

Another man answered: 'Because we are smarter.'

There was general merriment at this; the man who had pronounced these words looked so much like a ram, and not a very bright one at that.

The older man turned back. 'I told you, my dear, they consider us foreigners, not Hungarians.'

'But to them the Gypsies are just as foreign.'

A new voice chimed in: 'That's right, we should all go and make music at the tavern instead of being company directors, and then we would not be persecuted.'

'Gentlemen, gentlemen, please,' interjected another comrade, who had a drugstore on the Boulevard. 'The problem is that we are a minority everywhere. Look at the Armenians in Turkey, or the Indians in America: the weaker have always and everywhere been persecuted and murdered.'

'Well, it's not such a simple matter.' (This came from Bank Director D., who had converted to Christianity.) 'It is a matter of religion usually.'

'But it did not help us to convert.'

'You see, you shouldn't have converted! A man of character does not convert!' said a slender little man, with passion. One side of his face twitched uncontrollably.

At this outburst the group became noisy. At least twenty voices were heard in more or less loud competition.

One elderly gentleman raised his arm.

'Gentlemen, may we have quiet!'

The word 'Zionist' was heard, and the little man with the tic shouted:

'That's right, I am a Zionist! That is the only road for the Jews!'

Again there was a loud hubbub, in the midst of which the little man responded to some comment in his excited voice:

'My son will! He will emigrate! I am not a narrow-minded orthodox Jew. Actually I am a freethinker. This, gentlemen, is a national problem. You don't have the slightest notion of Zionism!'

Again, the loud outbursts were calmed by requests for quiet.

Someone, I couldn't see who, exclaimed indignantly:

'But I converted out of conviction!'

'That's right, you were convinced that it would be to your advantage!'

Laughter, and another hubbub. The old gentleman calling for order was almost in tears.

'Gentlemen! Gentlemen!'

A bent, blond-haired man with a tired face said to no one in particular:

'I have nothing to do with this! I was born a Christian.'

The little man with the tic laughed as he pointed at the other man's chest:

'And look, they still gave you a star.'

'But even with that star I went to church every Sunday. I am a practising Catholic.'

The man with the tic waved him off and left.

The older man, who had started it all, looked at me.

'And what a wasted martyrdom this is, what a ridiculous affair! So we are to be only Jews, after all? We are also

Hungarians, and human beings. Oh, to be persecuted for one's religion, in Europe, in our day . . .'

Situation Report

Again we had encouraging word from the office, promising release on the morrow for those with passes and people over sixty.

Every day we had been pining away from morning till noon, from noon till nightfall. And then we laid down our heads again.

For the past week we had been receiving only a quarter of a kilo of bread per person every other day. This was our chief nourishment. And what miserable bread it was; one's finger poked holes in its heavy, yellow-grey muck.

Personally I couldn't complain because at the kitchen they always helped me out with a piece of relatively edible bread.

Yesterday I gave half my bread to a landowner who used to possess more than 10,000 acres of first-rate wheatland in Hungary's breadbasket.

Kind Albert Havas kept surprising me with snippets of smoked bacon and an occasional bite of sausage, or an apple or pear. I never knew where he obtained these.

A soldier arrived from Budapest with the news that the Germans had blown up Margaret Bridge on the Danube.* It had not been reported in the daily paper, and we did not believe him. That kind of news was impossible to believe.

---

* The Germans blew up all of the Budapest bridges during the 1944 siege.

By now, the gentlemen's shirts were not exactly spot-less. It was hard to do laundry here. Their nails were not cared for, either. This was a symptom of something beyond exhaus-tion and apathy: maybe the liberation of the child trapped in our souls, and some kind of nostalgia drifting us towards the condition and lot of the wild Patagonian.

And beautiful beards could be seen: some resembled Henry V, others were Christ-like.

The Germans

It was on the twelfth day, I think, when two or three German armoured cars and about twenty trucks clattered into our compound. You may imagine how quiet all of the earth-workers became when they saw this upon their arrival after work.

The vehicles had been brought here for repair. The Germans, who had a captain among them, stayed for four days.

The next morning when that captain walked past the drying loft he noticed an asthmatic old man sitting in the sun on a pile of bricks. He had been given the doctors' permission to stay behind. The captain, who was a young man, turned back after he had passed the old man, and asked him what the matter was. Then he proceeded back to his quarters and returned ten minutes later with a bottle of red wine and a jar of jam, which he gave to the old gentleman.

On the morning after, when our earthworkers were marching off to work, two of the German soldiers were stand-ing by the gate. One, a big, heavy sergeant built like a

Mecklenburg dray horse, kept shouting at them as they passed by:

'Arbeitet, Mistviehe! Arbeitet nur, Mistviehe!' ('Work, shitbirds! Just work, shitbirds!')

The other German yelled:

'Juda verrecke! Juda verrecke!' ('Jews, it's reckoning time!')

Just like back in the early days of the Hitler era.

But there were Germans, both privates and non-commissioned officers, who stopped to talk with the Jews and handed out cigarettes.

Back in 1940 when I lived on Margaret Island, Gräfin von Einsiedel, a charming German woman of sixty, looked me up. She brought a message from Herr Wagenseil in Berlin, who was involved with translating and placing my work. He wanted some of my short stories and my latest books; he was willing to publish them, under a pseudonym for the time being. The countess, by pulling strings, had been able to obtain a four-week pass to come to Budapest, ostensibly for a rheumatic cure. Actually there was nothing wrong with her, except that, as she put it:

'Vier Wochen lang wollt ich wieder ein Mensch sein.' ('For four weeks I'll feel like a human being again.')

This woman described to me how others who felt the way she did had organized networks in several districts, with the aid of the more decent policemen and mailmen, to smuggle food packages to Jews. She also told me how they were typing up secret editions of Heine's works, how his *Buch der Lieder* and *Romanzero* were being passed around in typed versions all over the Reich.

She added that they were the most wretchedly misunderstood ones, those Germans who were not Nazis, but who would be equated with the Nazis by the rest of the world. If only I could imagine how sick it made her to go out every day to hear those shouts of '*Heil Hitler!*' and see that moronic raising of paws. For that reason, she went out as little as possible.

There were Jews, even here among us, who were incorrigible Germanophiles. They constantly spouted off about *Farbenindustrie* and Sollingen and Zeiss, and German order and German industriousness and cleanliness, and of course Goethe and Wagner and Beethoven. And Koch and Behring! It was a bitter blow to them to see Germany so misled. They kept repeating, and I had heard this for years, that Hitler's setting the Germans against the Jews (to obtain a cheap victory) would prove his downfall. If, on the contrary, he had recruited the gifted, industrious Jews on his side, he would have won an inestimable propaganda victory, and would have obtained Danzig and the former German colonies without bloodshed. He would not have taken over Vienna and Prague; there would have been no war.

During dinner (not burnt, for a change), the former professor at the University of Halle turned to one of the Germanophiles among us.

'Forgive me, sir, but it seems to me your heart is bleeding because the Germans will lose this war and stars in the firmament will not line up two by two.'

This professor had been dragged off from home with his broken leg still unhealed. On the march here we had been afraid that he would not make it and would be shot on the road.

Of course, there were among us those who felt all Germans should be wiped off the face of the earth.

As for me, I don't consider Goethe to be a German: he is Goethe. Nor is Beethoven a German: he is Beethoven. They were sent by the Almighty to make the German people more humane.

According to the professor, the Germans have three sins: their cigarettes are unsmokable, their soups inedible, and they somehow even manage to spoil coffee.

Myself, I look for the exceptions among the Germans, those who are innocent. But I must admit that I can no longer stand the sight of Gothic script. It bristles with bayonets.

On the way up to the loft after dinner, the Germanophile gentleman fired a parting shot at the professor.

'In a hundred years, the world will be run by Germans. You'll see, professor.'

'I will? That ought to be something!'

You see, we had our lighter moments.

We're Going Home at Last

Yes, the following evening an officer was to come from Csomád and bring the approved list of exemptions: people with passes, the seriously ill and those over sixty. This officer would issue our discharge papers and we would be off that very night. At last. It would be a little easier marching homeward.

Well, the next day came, and went. But we were still there. It seemed they had forgotten about us at Csomád.

Instead of the officer, we had a visit from a military surgeon, who examined the sick. He left them alone. Few of the inmates at Erdőváros could be pronounced healthy, anyway.

Herr Direktor T., who had endeavoured so assiduously on our behalf, tried to console us. The office was overloaded with work; if they did not come today, they would come for us tomorrow.

But they didn't.

Every day we grew more impatient and miserable, after a whole week of thinking this would be our last night lying down on the brick floor. Again, and yet again, we had to climb up to that awful loft.

Just a Little More Patience

My poor reader, how boring this all must be.

But as you can see, it is almost over; only a few more pages are left.

All this uncertainty was extremely painful, as was the forced idleness.

All day I loitered, looking on at the workers, chatting with some. There was a black puppy in the kitchen but he didn't stay around much, he preferred to go off on his own to chase hares.

I had asked several of the forced labourers how they managed without women.

One of them said he was so dead beat each night he had not even thought about women.

Another seconded this; he was of the opinion that even women were a matter of habit. He did admit to occasional wet dreams, but these were less and less frequent.

Another man, 33 and married, thought that abstinence was a matter of mental discipline. He swore emphatically, without my asking him about this, that he had not masturbated in the eight months he had been here. He would have considered that an infidelity.

One spoke about waking up at night to hear his neighbour sobbing; the man was crying for his wife. I heard it said that several of them had their wives under observation back home. One of them had a Gentile woman for a sweetheart; he too was insanely jealous and had her watched.

In the course of a political chat with one of our older invalids, I heard a neat little summary:

'Hungary may be described in one sentence. The peasants blame the gentry, the gentry blame the Jews, and the Jews blame each other.'

At night I sometimes turned on the wrong side in my sleep, and my wounded hand would throb all morning.

In the evening I overheard two gentlemen reminiscing in chow line. One, whose face was familiar to me from Tarján's Café, said:

'I'll describe what used to be my favourite menu in Budapest: Perch-trout à la Mornay, sautéed veal, sautéed potatoes, with Debrecen sausages and goose liver added (and here he gave a sigh of pain and pleasure); and then, an "omelette surprise", and for cheese, a Gervais. For drinks, I used to start with a cocktail, then a glass of beer, followed by my special wine, a Riesling, Festetich vineyards (here a loud smacking of the lips); and I always had a snort of Benedictine with my coffee. Do you think we will ever eat like that again? My heart aches, my friend, when I think of those bygone nights.'

The other replied:

'And how! As for me, my dear, I went in for good old Hungarian-style cuisine. Listen to this dinner menu: Noodle and potato soup, pan-roasted steak, cabbage strudel, perhaps some egg dumplings, and my cheese was Brie, but it had to be runny! Regarding cheese, I am a partisan of the French. There is nothing like Brie in this whole wide world. Well, what do you say, did a Vanderbilt ever eat like that?'

The other gentleman, after a moment's pause, replied in melancholy accents:

'And what would you have by way of drinks?'

I saw a large, husky gentleman pacing about the yard before dinnertime, gnawing on something. What do you think it was? A raw potato. He saw me looking at him, and stopped by my side.

'Look what I found. It has a lot of vitamins in it.'

There are some poor people in rags among us who are fat. They are starving, but they still have their bulk. A starving man who is fat is a very sad sight, because he receives no pity.

And we still had our constantly weeping wretch, and the one who walked about all day in wordless prayer, eyes looking up to heaven over his clasped hands, and our autistic man who stood all day in the loft, staring at the straw. Just like so many actors, doomed to the same performance night after night.

The sponging artist discovered a new approach. He had a way of bumming a cigarette even from those with whom he had quarrelled. He asked for the smoke wordlessly, by placing two fingers to his lips and inhaling. If he received a cigarette, he moved on without a word of thanks.

By taking a militant stance with the doctors he had wormed his way among the seriously ill who would be sent home.

There was a sad faction among us: people who stood or walked in the yard, in a solitary trance far from their companions.

During my nights of torment I consoled myself with the thought that I would write about our vicissitudes, and they would be of some interest in retrospect. But what about these others who suffered blindly, the ones without any recourse; how were they to find relief and consolation? I used to feel the same pity in civilian life for those who had been disappointed in love: instead of writing poems or novels, they turned to suicide.

I too stood around in a trance at times, tormented by the sins of this world. I would stand for ten or fifteen minutes at a time, unaware of what I was doing. The war filled my head, without my having to think of it. Oh, I should have been able to get these thoughts out of my head during the First War. This second time around I was suffering without my heart being in it, as it were; as if my heart had burned itself out and ossified during that First War. And ever since then my mind has been in chaos. I still have not given an accounting of that time, before men and before God. It is as if I have been in hiding ever since, cheating and lying with each one of my words, each glance, each breath.

Even now, just as in that First War, I was utterly amazed at times: how dare they do this, what they are doing, how dare they, when I am here as a witness who can see and hear everything. Why aren't they dumbfounded, ashamed; how can they go on with this?

These were the thoughts that assailed me with the burning torment of madness.

And I was haunted by another thought, and still am: that I was the cause of it all, I was the one to blame. The Creator had endowed me with a heart, and sent me down among the people. And I could not fathom how it had happened that I had not shown everyone my heart, their heart. Had I been asleep all this time? Waiting here in my throat was the life-saving word, the redeemer; the word that would command joyfulness on Earth. And I had remained silent.

I don't know where my attention strayed. I had let go of the world, and it had broken into pieces.

Adieu, Bricks

Two days went by, then four more, then six.

Meanwhile the dreadful news came that the Chain Bridge had been blown up.*

On the third day this news proved to be false, for now. But the news about Margaret Bridge, alas, turned out to be true. One of the forced labourers who had been sent to town had seen it.

The next day we heard that the Russians were as close as Soroksár. Panic seized us. If the Russians encircled Budapest, we would not be sent home.

During those days we had hoped that the Germans and the Arrow Cross would have evaporated by then, and we would be free to go where we pleased.

Then came the alarming rumour that we were to be taken west. The next day, word came from the office that this was not the case.

I think it was the day after that when, on 8 November, miracle of miracles, an officer, accompanied by a few soldiers, at last arrived from Csomád to let us go.

He arrived in the afternoon, and had a large deal table set up in front of the lower building, where half of us had been quartered.

After dinner all of us with protective passes had to line up over there. Certified disabled veterans and those in the munitions industry were also included, thanks to the fact that the regular army had taken us over from the Arrow Cross. (Captain Megay might have had something to do with this.)

So the lieutenant examined everyone's documents in

* The oldest bridge (completed in 1848) linking Buda and Pest. Blown up in 1944, it was the first to be rebuilt after the war.

the light of a lamp at that table, and filled out our discharge papers. We had to stand in line for a long time, but it was worth it.

The ailing were ordered to report at the office. Inside, a lengthy struggle ensued between our doctors and the army doctor from Csomád. The latter wanted to permit only a small percentage to return home, while our doctors fought for each patient.

Yes, I was going home, thanks to my Swedish papers.

When we went back to the loft, our two company commanders read out the names of those over sixty who were scheduled to go home. Well, more than a few were in for a rude shock. For, according to the Csomád command, only those who had passed their sixty-first birthday were considered to be over sixty.

Engineer Marton revealed that the rest of the company, those not returning to Budapest, were to be taken to Békásmegyer at midnight. We who were going home had to rise at 4 a.m. and report at the Veresegyház station at six. Because of the invalids among us, we were to go by train.

Our commander (who never gave any commands) ended by giving a moving little speech. He apologized for any offence he might have given, and reminded us never to forget each other. Those who had quarrelled should make up now; he would keep the list of our names and addresses and the engineers, our former commanders, would call us for occasional reunions, as befits comrades. He also appointed a small delegation to visit poor Endre Frank's widow. And we should all have on hand four pengős fifty in the morning for our third-class train fare. He would be happy to lend the money to anyone who needed it.

The engineer K., the other company's commander, also spoke, and received a fine ovation.

We said our goodbyes to those who had to go on to Békásmegyer. We expressed the usual hopes that, etc., etc.

Next morning at four-fifteen all of us were down by the well. For the first time there was no pushing and shoving. Again there was no water, only a little dark-grey puddle at the bottom of the well. This was shared, and people ended up washing in the blackened left-over portions of others.

Needless to say our artist friend was going home with us. My last cigarette was smoking in his mouth. We received no coffee this morning. As for bread, this was the fourth day we had not had any. But who cared about this last bit of starvation.

The forced labourers came to see us off and to send messages and letters to Budapest. Albert Havas also appeared, and brought me a fine ear of roast corn. Poor man, he had to stay behind.

We had an escort of five or six regular army soldiers, my 'kinsman' Péter Pál Szép among them. He was such a bright and lively fellow. Right away he offered his services to the gentlemen from Pozsonyi Road: he would see us to our door to make sure none of us would be harrassed on the way.

For the past three days word had it that the Arrow Cross men had made themselves scarce on the streets of Budapest, and most of them had taken off to the west, along with the Germans.*

We did not know what to believe.

We lined up, and marched out. On the way to the gate we passed the last sad piles of bricks. These were fine, hard bricks, clinkers, pale pink in hue like the cheeks of young

---

* The siege of Budapest proved to be a bloody battle lasting nearly three months, taking a terrible toll on the civilian population. In addition, atrocities and random killings by Arrow Cross thugs took the lives of many Jews confined to the ghetto.

maidens. The sun was not yet up, so these bricks were all the more melancholy and wan. Bricks too must have a soul; if they don't, I hereby give it to them. These bricks had to stay here and wait and wait in utter boredom. How they would have loved to hear the sound of the bricklayer's hammer, how they would have loved to be placed in the façade of some fine and homely new building, how they would have loved to drop on someone's head. Well, so long, bricks of Erdőváros; too bad you could not become Swedish and come with us.

At Veresegyház we were squeezed into a train with not enough carriages. We were dropped off at Rákospalota, from where streetcars took us to the Western Railway Station.

In front of our entrance, Péter Pál Szép received a 100-pengő note from each gentleman. Mr Aczél even offered to treat him to a free suit, once the Indestructible shop was open for business.

It was the ninth of November when we got home. I will not go on to narrate what happened starting on the tenth. That, I feel, is not to be described, not to be believed.

And even what I have narrated here, even this, 'if you want, remember, if you want, forget'.*

---

* These last words are in English in the original.

A Note on Dezső Tandori

Born in Budapest in 1938, Dezső Tandori is the author of more than thirty volumes of poetry and prose, beginning with the 1968 selection of poems, *Töredék Hamletnek* ('A Fragment for Hamlet'). In addition, he is a well-known translator and a graphic artist. Starting in the late 1970s, sparrows and other birds, raised and cared for by the writer and his wife, became a main theme of Tandori's writings, by providing a unique opportunity to reflect upon the possibility of play and flights of spirit in the face of the usual human tasks, responsibilities and intimations of mortality. A selection of Tandori's poetry, *Birds and Other Relations*, translated by Bruce Berlind, was published by Princeton University Press in 1986.

A Note on the Translator

John Batki, poet, translator and kilimologist, was born in Miskolc, Hungary, but has lived in the United States since the age of fourteen. He studied art and literature at Columbia and Syracuse universities, has published short stories in *The New Yorker* and FICTION, received the O. Henry Award, and taught at Harvard and Syracuse. As a translator of twentieth-century Hungarian literature, his publications include the poems of Attila József, a collection of novellas by Iván Mándy, Miklós Mészöly and Géza Ottlik, and Péter Lengyel's novel *Cobblestone*. In 1993 he was a Fulbright Research Fellow in Budapest, translating the fiction of Iván Mándy.